100 YEARS OF ADVERTISING IN BRITISH AVIATION

IMMEDIATE POST-WAR DISPOSITION OF MAJOR AIRCRAFT AND ENGINE CONSTRUCTORS

1. The de Havilland Aircraft Co Ltd (Airspeed Division), The Airport, Portsmouth

2. The de Havilland Aircraft Co Ltd (Airspeed Division), Christchurch Aerodrome, Hampshire

3. Alvis Ltd, Holyhead Road, Coventry

4. Armstrong Siddeley Motors Ltd, Coventry

5. Sir W G Armstrong Whitworth Aircraft Ltd, Baginton, Nr Coventry

6. Auster Aircraft Ltd, Rearsby Aerodrome, Rearsby, Leicester

7. Blackburn and General Aircraft Ltd, Brough, East Yorkshire

8. Blackburn (Dumbarton) Ltd, Dumbarton

9. Boulton Paul Aircraft Ltd, Pendeford Lane, Wolverhampton

10. The Bristol Aeroplane Co Ltd, Aircraft and Engine Divisions, Filton House, Bristol

11. The de Havilland Aircraft Co Ltd, Hatfield, Hertfordshire

12. The de Havilland Aircraft Co Ltd, Broughton, Nr Chester

13. The de Havilland Engine Co Ltd, Stag Lane, Edgware, Middlesex

14. The de Havilland Engine Co Ltd, Leavesden, Nr Watford, Hertfordshire

15. Elliotts of Newbury Ltd, Albert Works, Newbury

16. The English Electric Co Ltd, Preston, Lancashire

17. The Fairey Aviation Co Ltd, Hayes, Middlesex

18. The Fairey Aviation Co Ltd, Heaton Chapel, Stockport, Cheshire

19. The Fairey Aviation Co Ltd, Hamble, Nr Southampton, Hampshire

20. The Fairey Aviation Co Ltd, White Waltham Aerodrome, Berkshire

21. Folland Aircraft Ltd, Hamble, Southampton

22. Gloster Aircraft Co Ltd, Gloucester

23. Handley Page Ltd, Cricklewood, London, NW2

24. Handley Page (Reading) Ltd, Woodley Aerodrome, Reading Berks

25. Hawker Aircraft Ltd, Canbury Park Road, Kingston on Thames, Surrey

26. Hawker Aircraft (Blackpool) Ltd, South Shore, Blackpool

27. Hunting Aircraft Ltd, Luton Airport, Bedfordshire

28. D Napier & Son Ltd, Acton, London, W3

29. D Napier & Son Ltd, Luton Airport, Bedfordshire

30. A V Roe & Co Ltd, Greengate, Middleton, Manchester

31. Rolls-Royce Ltd, Derby

32. Rolls-Royce Ltd, Hillington, Glasgow

33. Saunders-Roe Ltd, Osborne, East Cowes, Isle of Wight

34. Saunders-Roe Ltd, Eastleigh

35. Scottish Aviation Ltd, Prestwick Aerodrome, Ayrshire

36. Short Bros & Harland Ltd, Queen's Island, Belfast

37. Slingsby Sailplanes Ltd, Kirbymoorside, York

38. Vickers-Armstrongs (Aircraft) Ltd, Weybridge, Surrey

39. Vickers-Armstrongs (Aircraft) Ltd, Supermarine Works, Hursley Park, Winchester, Hampshire

40. Westland Aircraft Ltd, Yeovil, Somerset

100 YEARS OF ADVERTISING IN BRITISH AVIATION

COLIN CRUDDAS

Right: An advertisement which truly encapsulates what this book is about is this August 1939 entry in *Flight*. It almost goes without saying that the Helliwell promotional series was a great favourite of the author and no doubt many thousands of other impressionable young men at the time!

This book is dedicated to all my ex-colleagues within the aerospace industry and to the multitude of artists who portrayed it so well.

First published 2008

The History Press
The Mill
Brimscombe Port
Stroud
Gloucestershire
GL5 2QG
www.thehistorypress.co.uk

British Library Cataloguing in Publication Data.
A catalogue record for this book is available from the British Library.

isbn 978-0-7524-4527-4

Typesetting and origination by The History Press Ltd
Printed in Malta

CONTENTS

ACKNOWLEDGEMENTS

The production of this book has been made possible by the many people who kindly contributed their valuable time, skills and material. Most, but not all, can look back on long careers within the aviation industry and I can say with confidence that it took little persuasion on my part to rally their support for my nostalgic reflections. My sincere thanks, therefore, go most particularly to my arch collaborators, Peter Amos (the Miles Aircraft Collection) and Dave Robinson along with:

Colin Ashford, Guild of Aviation Artists
Christopher Balfour
Fred Ballam, AgustaWestland
Eric Barker, BAE Systems Heritage (Brough)
John Blake, Guild of Aviation Artists
George Burton, Miles Aircraft Collection
Tony Buttler
Tony Clark
Jim Davis, British Airways Museum
Peter Elliott, Royal Air Force Museum
John Elver, Rolls-Royce Heritage Trust
Mike Fielding, BAE Systems Heritage (Farnborough)
Harry Fraser-Mitchell, Handley Page Association
Richard Gardner, Farnborough Air Sciences Trust
Steve Gillard, BAE Systems Heritage (Brough)
Paul Gladman, *Flight International* magazine
Duncan Greenman, Bristol Air Chive

Barry Guess, BAE Systems Heritage (Farnborough)
Patrick Hassell, Rolls-Royce Heritage Trust
Dave Hatchard, Solent Sky Museum
Harry Holmes, Avro Heritage Centre
David Howie, Rolls-Royce plc
Ian Huntley, The Fairey Archive
Paul Jarvis, British Airways Museum
Alan Jones, Solent Sky Museum
Albert Kitchenside, Brooklands Museum
Amy Rigg, Emily Locke and Glad Stockdale, The History Press
Alan McKnight, Bombardier Aerospace (Shorts), Belfast
Paul McMaster, Ulster Aviation Society
Mick Oakey, *Aeroplane* magazine
Norman Parker, A and AEE Boscombe Down Archive
Peter Skinner, Croydon Airport Society
Ron Smith, BAE Systems
Colin van Geffen, Solent Sky Museum
Guy Warner, Ulster Aviation Society
Dave Whatley, Solent Sky Museum
Larry Williamson, Croydon Airport Society

I am especially grateful to BAE Systems plc, AgustaWestland, Rolls-Royce plc, British Airways Museum, the RAF Museum and *Flight International* and *Aeroplane* magazines for granting me such wide copyright clearance. My heartfelt thanks also go to the talented artists, photographers and graphics designers, many now sadly departed, whose works, commissioned by the companies, were such an integral part of Britain's leading aviation press. Had it been possible to do so, I would certainly have listed all these wonderfully creative people on a 'roll of honour' within this book. That so many remained anonymous, or appended just initials or indecipherable signatures to their works, has unfortunately made this impossible!

Two ladies have also earned my immense thanks for their unstinting efforts. Firstly, Julia Liddle, for her patient and impressively prompt word processing; and secondly, my wife, Thelma, whose proof-reading and text improvement skills have, as always, proved invaluable. I am also indebted to the country's premier aviation historian Phil Jarrett and to Graham Skillen, an ex-colleague from Concorde's flight development days in the 1970s, for casting their critical eyes on the book's technical and historical accuracy.

Finally, I must thank Cobham plc's erstwhile chairman, Mr Gordon Page CBE, for writing the foreword. His long and distinguished family association with aviation have placed him at the very centre of the modern industry and I value greatly his introductory comments.

Colin Cruddas
Shaftesbury, 2008

FOREWORD

I am delighted to introduce this fascinating book to you for it takes a distinctly different look at the development of aviation in the UK over the last 100 years.

The story, since Samuel Cody's first powered flight at Farnborough on 16 October 1908, is reflected in a wide selection of aviation advertisements which embrace the major constituent elements of aviation – undoubted glamour, and engineering advancement that has always been pioneering, exciting and risky. These evocative illustrations also reflect the large number and variety of companies which have played a significant part in the evolvement of aviation in this country. Most have now disappeared entirely or have been absorbed into the large consolidated companies of the twenty-first century.

Many of these advertisements are works of art in their own right. They also show their own technological development – from black and white to colour, from artists' impressions to photographs. The author has clearly mastered a very difficult job of selection and I thoroughly recommend this most interesting and informative book to you.

G.F. Page CBE DL FRAeS
Chairman, Cobham plc (2001–2008)

G.F. Page.

INTRODUCTION

On 16 October 1908, an American, Samuel Franklin Cowdery (who preferred to use the surname of his Wild West hero, Cody), made the first officially recognised powered aeroplane flight in Great Britain.

Join me now, if you will, on a nostalgic journey through the 100 years of British aviation that have elapsed since that memorable event. Not, I hasten to add, via a detailed accounting of technical advancement and achievement. My much simpler aim has been to follow the evolution of the industry through the uniqueness of its advertising. In other words, to let the wonderfully evocative artworks so frequently featured on and within the covers of the trade press and elsewhere become our guide. Here, I would point out that some companies warrant the inclusion of far more examples of the high-quality work they commissioned than other, equally famous firms that were seemingly less inclined to broadcast their wares.

Having bowed to my publisher's request to keep the illustration content down to manageable proportions, I apologise in advance for any 'unforgivable omissions'. I can only draw a parallel with the difficulty of trying to choose an all-time best team for any given sport – very much in the eye of the beholder!

In referring to the 'aircraft-aerospace industry', I've taken it to include not only the major airframe, engine and equipment manufacturers, but also the many and varied organisations which have, over the years, promoted and presented flying activities to the general public.

Few ex-employees of my vintage would disagree that Britain's heavily populated 'go it alone' aircraft manufacturing industry, such as it existed in the wartime and subsequent post-war periods, has now virtually disappeared. This is not to deny, however, the presence and influence of British brains and skills in today's global aerospace community.

This book, then, dwells on those years when many aviation companies, with names then easily recognised, offered distinctively designed products they were proud to advertise. In all fairness, it must be said that not all were 'world-beaters', for a good many projects were either stillborn or ended in failure due to political ineptitude, lack of capital investment (and hence the means to continue research) or simply because the cost of unit production could not compete with that in foreign countries.

A distinct parallel may be drawn between the development of advertising art in the separate but allied transportation fields of aviation, shipping and motoring. This is not surprising as several influential artists proved pre-eminent in more than one of these areas. The earliest examples of aviation advertising, *c.*1909, tended to rely on simple cartoon-like sketches to accompany basic text, but by the outbreak of the First World War these had largely given way to far more ornate, eye-catching illustrations supporting very detailed product descriptions.

Particularly appealing were the sophisticated art deco-style travel posters commissioned in the 1920s and 1930s by Imperial Airways. At the same time, the manufacturing companies continued to promote their products using prosaic half-tone illustrations alongside their more colourful neighbours. No doubt due to wartime economy and the call-up of talented staff, colour advertising tended to take a back seat during the 1939-45 period, although not entirely, for many of the dramatically illustrated posters introduced by the government to boost public morale were given full colour treatment for maximum effect.

During the twenty-five years or so following the end of the war, this form of advertising copy reached its peak, before then being overtaken by a general preference for a more 'down to earth' photographic format. Some firms still continued with half-tone impressions, but the old style artistic skills, along with those of the 'tee and set square' draughtsman in the design office, were being superseded by the highly flexible computer graphics package.

I have had to be very selective in my choice of advertising illustrations, and regrettably have had to put many fine artistic examples to one side. However, I feel that those that have been chosen best express the high hopes and aspirations of what became, over the past century, a vital and profitable national asset – the British aviation industry.

Times have now moved on and we shall not see the likes of these individual companies again, nor their diverse range of products or the need to advertise in what may now seem such a naive and simplistic manner. I hope, therefore, that you will enjoy these picturesque reminders of a largely bygone technical age as much as I have in putting them together.

GETTING OFF THE GROUND, 1908–1914

There can be few areas of invention in which the efforts to succeed rival man's attempts to emulate the birds. Certainly, there were more failures than successes between the advent of ballooning in 1783 and 1903, when the Wright brothers undertook their first powered flight, but the perseverance and dedicated work of the early pioneers such as the Yorkshire squire Sir George Cayley, William Samuel Henson and John Stringfellow, Thomas Walker, F.H. Wenham, J.W. Dunne and, a little later, Frederick Lanchester resolutely ensured scientific continuity in the pursuance of powered flight in this country. There were, of course, many others whose valiant efforts were not recorded for posterity!

By the mid-1800s, the first aeronautical societies were established in France (1863) and Britain (1866), and in 1868 the world's first aero-exhibition was held at the Crystal Palace. Although at this time a great deal of attention was being given to the theory of flight, practical demonstration was greatly hindered by the lack of suitable means of propulsion. However, present-day assessments of the many proposed flying machines suggest it was indeed fortunate that a practical engine did not exist, for the ability to control an aerial vehicle was simply nowhere in sight. The work carried out by the Wright brothers changed all that, and their magnificent technical breakthrough, though initially disbelieved in Europe, proved to be the major springboard for aviation development. Word about the way forward in aeronautics was first broadcast in America as early as 1894, when Octave Chanute published his *Progress in Flying Machines*. Three memorable volumes were also published by another American, James Means, with his *Aeronautical Annual* in 1895–7, but it was undoubtedly the carefully recorded experiments of Wilbur and Orville Wright that defined the principal requirements for sustained, powered and controlled flight.

In France in 1906, the diminutive Brazilian, Alberto Santos-Dumont, already famous for his balloon and airship flights over Paris at the turn of the century, became the first to lay claim to heavier-than-air flight in Europe. Though his attempts were successful enough to win major prize money, the short distances covered would be barely regarded today as 'proper' flights. His tail-first biplane, 14-bis, lacked any effective form of control and, after having carried out several ambitious straightforward hops, the longest being 220 metres, it never flew again.

In 1908 at Le Mans, Wilbur Wright astounded Europe's aeronautical pioneers by demonstrating his Flyer's ability to perform turns, banks, climbs, figures-of-eight and to remain in the air for over an hour. This revolutionary exhibition provided the necessary 'wake-up call' for continental designers, and within a year they had achieved technical parity with the Wright brothers who, greatly concerned with patent protection for their hard-won method of three-axis flight control, also now found their pre-eminence threatened by other inventive aviators in the United States, such as Glenn Curtiss. An Englishman (later a naturalised Frenchman), Henri Farman, and a French counterpart, Louis Blériot, then produced machines which, powered by 8-cylinder, 50hp rotary engines such as the Gnome, led to notable cross-country flights, and the crossing by Blériot, albeit then employing a 3-cylinder 25hp Anzani engine, of the English Channel in July 1909.

With the world's first air meeting held at Rheims later that year, at which four biplanes and two monoplanes were on sale to the public, the aeroplane, though still rudimentary, dangerous and unreliable, could be said to have arrived!

In Britain at this time, aeronautical progress had largely centred on balloon development, with cautious interest being shown by the Army. The success of the Wrights in France, however, persuaded the Short brothers, Horace, Eustace and Oswald, then the country's leading balloon manufacturers, to consider the commercial promise of heavier-than-air machines. Accordingly, after forming a new company, Short Brothers, in 1908, they acquired a licence to build six Short-Wright Flyers. In so doing, they not only secured the first aircraft production contract (worth £8,400) but became the world's first aircraft manufacturing company. Remarkably, considering the seismic industrial upheavals that have taken place since then, 'Shorts', now located in Belfast, is still a name that features prominently within the aerospace fraternity, as part of the Canadian Bombardier Aerospace organisation.

With practical flight now a reality, Britain began to produce its own flying adventurers. It was at the first Model Aeroplane Competition promoted by Lord Northcliffe's *Daily Mail* in 1907 that Alliott Verdon Roe, who was later to found the Avro Company, won the chief award of £75 for his soundly designed biplane. He put this money towards the building of a canard biplane in which he managed a few short flights under tow at Brooklands in 1907-8. More success was had with his next machine, the Roe I triplane, and on 23 July 1909 at Lea Marshes, Essex, he became the first Briton to fly an all-British aeroplane, though only for 300 yards.

Just weeks earlier, on 14 May, Samuel Cody had achieved the distinction of being the first to fly over 1 mile in Britain, and landed without breaking anything. Highly impressed, the Prince of Wales asked Cody to repeat his feat later the same afternoon, but he was less fortunate this time and, in turning to avoid a troop column, crashed into an embankment and severely damaged his aeroplane. Cody had first arrived on the European scene with the intention of touring the provincial music-halls as a 'Wild West' sharpshooter, but it was after he visited England in 1899, following hugely successful stage appearances on the continent, that a long-dormant interest in kite-flying was reawakened. By 1904, he had designed, built and demonstrated to the Admiralty and the Army a succession of man-carrying variants suitable for observation or signalling purposes. These attracted little official interest, not least because of Cody's theatrical insistence on appearing with shoulder-length hair, black Stetson and ground length coat whilst riding a magnificent white stallion!

Although the military was unimpressed with Cody's presentational style, the general public greeted his flamboyant endeavours with enormous enthusiasm. Eventually the War Office relented and allowed the Royal Engineers at the Aldershot Balloon School to re-apprise his War Kite. This led to his engagement as the Army's kite instructor and, because of his new commitments, the closing down of his profitable family involvement with the theatre.

Cody's expertise was recognised and encouraged by Lieutenant Colonel John Capper, then in charge of airship development at the Farnborough Balloon Factory, and who then involved him in the completion of the British Army Dirigble No.1, Nulli Secundus, an airship project initiated by Capper's predecessor, Colonel J. Templer. The airship made its first flight from Farnborough on 10 September 1907. On 5 October it over flew and circled St Paul's Cathedral. However, the return against stiff headwinds caused engine overheating and a forced descent at Crystal Palace, prematurely ending what was undoubtedly a momentous event in British aviation.

Cody then turned his attention, with Capper's full support, to the power plant installation for an aeroplane. After a great deal of research and experimentation, and following several tentative hops, he finally achieved a true flight of 1,390ft on 16 October 1908, which, verified by impartial witnesses, was thereafter regarded as the first officially recorded powered flight in Great Britain.

By now, securing notable aviation 'firsts' had become the order of the day and, again, just ahead of A.V. Roe's 'all British claim', J.T.C. Moore-Brabazon (later Lord Brabazon of Tara) won a place in the record books with three flights between 30 April and 2 May 1909, making him the first resident Englishman

to achieve an officially recognised flight in England. These took place at Leysdown on the Isle of Sheppey in (note the critical difference to A.V. Roe's endeavour) a French-built Voisin biplane. Shortly afterwards he carried out a well-advertised flight with a pig in a basket to prove the old adage that 'pigs might fly' – this one certainly did! Moore-Brabazon also gained, though not without contention, the prestigious distinction of receiving the Aero Club of Great Britain's Aviator Certificate No.1 on 8 March 1910.

With flying increasingly gaining the public's sporting attention, entrepreneurs lost little time in cashing in. The first aviation meeting to be held in the country was organised by the Doncaster Aviation Committee on the town's racecourse between 15–23 October 1909. Not to be outdone by their Yorkshire neighbours, the first officially recognised meeting was jointly promoted over virtually the same period by Blackpool Corporation and the Lancashire Aero Club. Despite the weather being generally unkind, allowing only five aeroplanes each at Doncaster and Blackpool to become airborne, over 50,000 people attended each event!

Awareness of the future use of the aeroplane was slow to take root, with the military commanding élite steeped in cavalry traditions. Nevertheless, by 1912, the War Office was beginning to recognise the aeroplane as offering some promise as an aid to reconnaissance. Trials were then held at Larkhill on Salisbury Plain to determine which aircraft were best suited to various roles. Thirty-one machines were privately entered, but it was Cody's Military Trials Biplane that proved successful. However, it was the government's Royal Aircraft Factory B.E.2 (Blériot Experimental) flying *hors concours* which showed the best military potential. Notwithstanding this seemingly forward step, officialdom was recalcitrant in promoting the development of suitable equipment for British Service pilots, and two years passed before the War Office finally issued a memorandum listing the requirements for a single-seat scout, a two-seat reconnaissance aircraft and a heavy two-seat fighter.

Fortunately, progress was being made elsewhere, with the formation of instructional flying schools primarily in southern England, at Larkhill, Hendon and at Brooklands in Surrey. Air races were also being promoted, and skilled individuals were achieving fame mainly at their own expense by thrilling the crowds at local exhibitions up and down the country. Not least of these was Gustav Hamel, who also conducted a series of officially sponsored tests in which mail commemorating the coronation of King George V was carried by air between Hendon and Windsor Great Park in September 1911.

Claude Grahame-White first attracted national attention in 1910 in the race to win the *Daily Mail's* £10,000 prize for the first flight from London to Manchester, a distance of 183 miles. This enormous cash incentive encouraged Grahame-White, lagging behind his French arch-competitor, Louis Paulhan, to attempt aviation's first night flight over the final stage of the course. The fact that he still failed to beat Paulhan simply served to enhance his reputation in the eyes of the British public and, within a day, he became Britain's first real air hero. He went on to carry out a hugely profitable demonstration visit to America which enabled him, along with Louis Blériot and Sir Hiram Maxim, to create the London Aerodrome at Hendon. Unfortunately, this proved to be a venture ahead of its time and was not a financial success.

Sadly, but inevitably, the advance of aviation, both in this country and overseas, took a heavy toll of life and limb. The Hon. Charles Stewart Rolls became the first British pilot to lose his life when, on 12 July 1910, at the Bournemouth Aviation Week, his French-built Wright biplane suffered a structural failure in flight. Britain's foremost airman Samuel Cody, who, by now having become a naturalised British citizen, revelled in the honorary title of 'Colonel' conferred upon him by King George V, did not survive a crash at Farnborough on 7 August 1913. Larger than life, even in death, his demise was said by C.G. Grey, the editor of *The Aeroplane*, to be 'the greatest blow those connected with British aviation have ever felt'! That most charismatic of young aviators, Gustav Hamel, whose father had been physician to King Edward VII, again captured the nation's headlines in the spring of 1914, when he disappeared without trace into an English Channel fog. Many others, perhaps far less famous, also paid the price for flying machines that were less than airworthy due to design, manufacturing, maintenance or inspection inadequacies. All too often, suspect piloting techniques were inherited from instructors themselves barely qualified or experienced in the new 'third dimension' of the air. Despite these deficiencies, there was always a steady supply of enthusiastic and courageous young men, along with a smattering of adventurous young ladies, keen to take on the challenge of flight. Others, with a shrewd eye to business opportunities, began to lay down the commercial structure of an industry that would shortly be called upon to expand beyond their wildest expectations. In the north of England, Robert Blackburn, inspired after witnessing Wilbur Wright's flying at Le Mans, set about establishing a career in aviation. By 1911 he had designed, built and flown his first monoplane at Filey on the Yorkshire coast. Bentfield C. Hucks, who had accumulated plenty of useful experience as a mechanic and fledgling pilot with Grahame-White at Hendon, had also joined Blackburn, quickly becoming his leading test pilot. With growing success and contracts being awarded for B.E.2c aircraft for both the Royal Flying Corps and the Royal Naval Air Service, the Blackburn Aeroplane and Motor Company Limited was formally registered in June 1914, taking over an initial order from the Admiralty for twelve such machines received earlier by Robert Blackburn.

In parallel with Blackburn's progress were the efforts of Geoffrey de Havilland in Hampshire. It was at Seven Barrows in December 1909 that de Havilland eased his first aeroplane off the ground – but not for long.

Insufficiently strong, its frail wings soon collapsed and it crashed, fortunately leaving its pilot intact, but little else. De Havilland had more success with his second machine and, despite trailing slightly behind the very earliest pioneers, by the latter part of 1910 he was carrying his wife and eight-week old son, also Geoffrey, as passengers. It was the sale of de Havilland's No.2 biplane to the Balloon Factory at Farnborough, whose brief was extended to 'afford opportunities for aeroplaning', that provided a much-needed financial recovery. It was also a far-sighted move when the Balloon Factory offered permanent employment to de Havilland and his assistant, Frank Hearle, as designer/pilot and mechanic respectively. This opportunity for de Havilland to gain experience within a large organisation was to have a major influence on British aviation in the years to come.

Frederick Handley Page was another visionary who lost little time in seeing limitless possibilities within aviation. Trained as an electrical engineer, he, like Charles Richard Fairey, a contemporary student at Finsbury Technical College, was soon attracted to the new science of mechanically assisted flight. Both men would go on to create very large successful companies. Handley Page, a man of immense determination, constructed his Bluebird (almost) in time for the 1910 Aero Exhibition at Olympia, but after unsuccessful trials he set about rebuilding it for the next Olympia show.

Such, then, were some of the early trials and tribulations that beset not only the flying fraternity but the engineering and future business pioneers upon whose foresight the very future of the country was later to depend. It would, however, be most remiss in this short accounting of the pre-war period to gloss over the other industrialists who contributed so much to British aviation.

In 1910, Sir George White founded not one, but four companies that were eventually amalgamated within the Bristol Aeroplane Company Limited. It was one of these companies, the British and Colonial Aeroplane Company, with its headquarters at Filton, that promoted the early Bristol Flying Schools at Larkhill and Brooklands as well as producing the highly successful Boxkite biplane.

Another true pioneer was Thomas Octave Murdoch (TOM) Sopwith, who, though born into financially secure and socially privileged surroundings, became determined to make his future within the newly emerging aviation industry. After learning to fly, he set up the Sopwith Aviation Company with partners Fred Sigrist and an Australian assistant pilot, Harry Hawker, taking over a former skating rink in Kingston-upon-Thames for production in 1912.

British aviation took its first tentative steps in the peaceful Edwardian years, but the ominous war clouds that gathered over Europe in mid-1914 soon formed the background for a massive expansion in the nation's manufacturing and training facilities. The big story was already unfolding.

THE FLYING SCHOOLS

The advertising for flying tuition and exhibitions was, in the beginning, very rudimentary. However, as the industry began to take root and gain confidence, it promoted itself to the public with more adventurous artwork. By the outbreak of war, several leading schools and companies had, through the strength of their advertising, become names largely familiar to the British public, namely:

Aeronautical Syndicate Limited
Beatty School of Flying
Bournemouth Aviation Company
British Caudron Company
British and Colonial Aeroplane
　　Company Limited
Grahame-White Company
Hewlett and Blondeau School
New Forest Aviation School
Ruffy-Baumann School of Flying
Vickers Flying School

These were just some of the early flying schools that proliferated in the pre-war period, mainly at Hendon, Farnborough and on Salisbury Plain. It was at these locations that the seeds of Britain's emerging aviation industry were sown, with seventeen instructional schools active at Brooklands alone before the outbreak of war.

The British and Colonial Aeroplane Company, in particular, made an indelible impact on the country's aeronautical future, not only because of the quality of its flying schools at Larkhill and Brooklands, but also through the design and manufacture of what soon became 'Bristol' aircraft at Filton. Note, however, that the 'Bristol' biplane referred to in the 1910 advertisement is not the famed Boxkite that proved so successful for the company. Although, as the illustrations show, many companies were competing in the home counties, other excellent flying schools were springing up throughout the country, from Bournemouth and the New Forest in the south to Lake Windermere in the north-west.

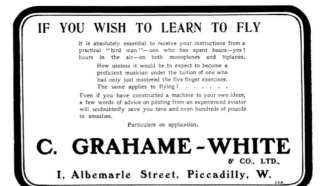

1

3

2

4

1　*Flight*, 11 June 1910.
2　*Flight*, 25 June 1910.
3　*Flight*, 25 June 1910.
4　*Aero*, 7 December 1910.
5　Source uncertain, *c.*1910.
6　*Aero*, 21 December 1910.
7　*Aero*, 8 March 1911.
8　*Flight*, 6 January 1914.
9　*The Aeroplane*, 8 January 1914.
10　*The Aeroplane*, 12 February 1914.
11　Source uncertain, *c.*1914.

THE PERSONAL TOUCH

When inducing the public to fly, buy or finance a project, advertising sometimes took on a personal appeal, as shown here. Despite Mr Neale's undoubted ability as a designer, his 'advanced' dirigible failed to attract the necessary support and he was not called upon to assist Britain's future war effort.

1　*Aero,* 19 October 1910.
2　*Aero,* 9 November 1910.
3　Source uncertain, *c.*1912.

THE LONG-LOOKED FOR

"CODY FLYER"

IS ON THE MARKET AT LAST.

35 h.p. 900 lbs. weight.　　55 h.p. 1,200 lbs. weight.

For the first time I express myself satisfied that my machine is sufficiently perfect to be offered for sale. I may have been a long time in producing this perfect article, but the fact is, I am hard to please. I shall be delighted to give likely purchasers a special flying display, with an All British practical machine.

———— Purchasers Taught to Pilot Free. ————

Construction undertaken to Clients' own designs. Workmanship, strength. and efficiency throughout, second to none.

Apprentices taken (Premium).　　　　　　　　　Pupils instructed.

Business Address: Aeroplane Shed, Laffan's Plane,
—— Farnborough, Hants. ——

Remember, I guarantee one hour flight with each "Cody Flyer."

1

NEALE
REQUIRES
£45,000
TO BUILD HIS
DIRIGIBLE
"NEALE II."

SPEED, Maximum	-	100 miles per hour
SPEED, Cruising -	-	20 " "
RANGE, at Maximum Speed	-	2,000 miles
RANGE, at Cruising Speed	-	10,940 "
LIFT, available for Fuel and Passengers	-	18 tons.

This Aerial Cruiser is primarily designed for the purposes of war and will carry quick-firing guns for protection against air craft. She will be fitted with search-lights, long range wireless equipment, telephotographic apparatus, and other modern implements for use in offensive and defensive tactics.

A few of these cruisers will at once give to Britain command of the air and place her in the fore-front of aerial navigation, instead of tamely following the lead of nations, who, at present, sell to us what their Governments do not require.

Mr. Neale is prepared to submit his design and data to a Committee of Experts for the information of those interested in the furtherance of the enterprise, which is not only necessary for our National welfare, but will also prove a sound commercial proposition.

NEALE'S AEROPLANE WORKS, Weybridge.
Telephone—267 Weybridge.　　　　　　Telegrams—"Neale, Weybridge."

2

3

THE AIR RACES AND DISPLAYS

Tremendous public interest was generated in the air displays, races and exhibitions held up and down the country in the pre-war years. Most popular were the events held at Brooklands and at Hendon's London Aerodrome where, for example, the first Aerial Derby, sponsored by the *Daily Mail,* in 1913 attracted more than 45,000 people. The advertising appears, on at least one occasion, to have become a little over-enthusiastic, showing a heroic, if terrified pilot about to meet his end!

1

2

3

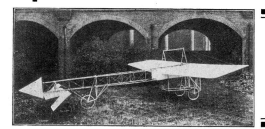

1

THE AIRCRAFT CONSTRUCTORS

The years prior to the First World War saw the founding of many companies that specialised in the production of either land or water-borne aircraft. This by no means exhaustive group of advertisements provides a good indication of the young, ambitious firms then confidently competing for sales. Howard T. Wright, for example, was an early innovative designer who, alongside the Short brothers, ranked as one of the very first British aircraft constructors. The advertisement shows a machine at his works under the London, Brighton and South Coast Railway arches at Battersea in 1910. After his company was absorbed into the Coventry Ordnance Works in 1912, Wright joined the shipbuilders J. Samuel White on the Isle of Wight.

1   *Flight,* 19 March 1910.

Handley Page Limited, formed in June 1909 and sited between Barking and Dagenham, was one of the first, soon-to-be large companies to advertise its products. In 1912, the firm was relocated to Cricklewood, where manufacturing continued until its closure in 1970.

1   *Flight,* 19 March 1910.

4

5

1   Official programme, 1913.
2   Local advertisement, 1913.
3   Official programme, 1914.
4   Official programme, 1914.
5   *The Aeroplane,* 5 March 1914.

1

Avro, destined to become one of the greatest names in British aviation, appeared first in 1910 as the Avro Flying School, and later, in 1913, as A.V. Roe and Company Limited. The growing strength of the company is reflected in the early 1914 advertisement for its 504 series of biplanes.

1 *Flight,* 12 March 1910.
2 *Flight,* c.1913.
3 *The Aeroplane,* 15 January 1914.

Sopwith Aviation Company was another firm which, from brave early beginnings, would go on through its progeny, Hawker, to become a major influential force in British aviation.

Sopwith's early advertisements, extolling the virtues of its Bat Boat (surprisingly not illustrated), were quickly overtaken by others depicting Howard Pixton's victory in the 1914 Schneider Cup race at Monaco, flying a Sopwith Tabloid seaplane.

1 *The Aeroplane,* 12 March 1914.
2 *The Aeroplane,* 30 April 1914.

Although most of Britain's early aviation progress took place in the south, Yorkshireman Robert Blackburn, highly influenced by the innovative French designers, produced a series of monoplanes in a small Leeds factory. In August 1913, the Blackburn Type 1 was delivered for flight testing, and it was this machine that featured in the company's advertisement shown here.

1 *The Aeroplane,* 12 March 1914.

Claude Grahame-White was, arguably, the best-known aviation 'all-rounder' in the run up to the First World War. In addition to his natural flying skills, evident at the early flying meetings and pageants, he set up a British Flying School at Pau in France, before concentrating on his own designs and transferring his instructional activities to Hendon.

1 *Flight,* 12 March 1910.
2 Source uncertain, *c.*1910.

Martin & Handasyde was a company with works in Camberwell that produced a series of monoplanes in the pre-war period. Later, it became the Martinsyde Aircraft Company, employing a young Sidney Camm, who later became chief designer at Hawker Aircraft.

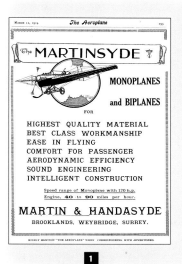

1 *The Aeroplane,* 12 March 1914.

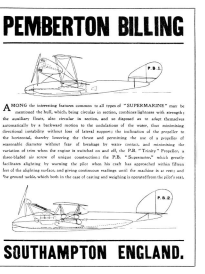

Though well known for his eccentric behaviour, Noel Pemberton Billing was highly regarded as a gifted and imaginative designer. Having formed Pemberton Billing in 1912, he engaged upon several projects that led to the Supermarine P.B.1 being displayed at the Aero and Marine Exhibition at Olympia in March 1914. More radical was his P.B.7 proposal for a flying-boat which, he claimed, if forced down onto the water, could shed its wings to allow the forward fuselage to act as a lifeboat.

Pemberton-Billing (note the latterly introduced hyphen) could, like T.O.M. Sopwith, lay claim to his original company having paved the way for a strong successor. Few would deny that Supermarine (having adopted the name of Pemberton-Billing's telegraphic address) was to serve Britain well in the years to come.

1 *Flight,* 11 April 1914.
2 *Flight,* 29 May 1914.

Short Bros, already well experienced in balloon-making, moved into airframe construction in 1909. In quickly securing the British rights to build an initial batch of six Wright Flyers for members of the Aero Club, it effectively launched the country's aircraft manufacturing industry. Although it continued to produce balloons and airship equipment, the firm consolidated its position as a major aircraft contractor by building seaplanes at a new factory at Rochester prior to the First World War.

1   *Flight,* 9 January 1909.
2   *Flight,* 12 March 1910.

Shipbuilders J. Samuel White, based on the Isle of Wight, were relative newcomers to aircraft design and manufacture. It was not until January 1913 and following the arrival of Howard T. Wright that an aviation department was set up to concentrate mainly on seaplanes which were advertised as 'Wight' machines.

1   *The Aeroplane,* 12 February 1914.

Adding to the increasing number of companies which produced their own entirely British designs, were several which acted as agents or manufacturers for established French companies such as Blériot, Deperdussin, Farman and Nieuport.

1

2

Not all the companies which started off with such high hopes survived. Humber, though advertising 'all-British excellence', soon relinquished its interest in aviation. White and Thompson, The Aircraft Company, The Twining Aeroplane Company and The Perry Aviation Company were just some of the early firms which, despite their confident claims, had faded from the scene by August 1914.

1 *Flight*, 1 January 1910.
2 *Aero*, 10 August 1910.

3

4

1 *Flight*, 9 April 1910.
2 *Flight*, 15 January 1910.
3 *Flight*, 15 February 1913.
4 *The Aeroplane*, 28 March 1914.

THE ENGINE MAKERS

Most of the pre-war British machines incorporated engines originally designed on the continent by the Gnome, Salmson, Renault, Clerget or Austro-Daimler companies. However, British firms were soon producing these under licence or marketing their own products.

The Anglo-French London and Parisien Motor Company with E.N.V. motors designed in England (but initially built in France), and those conceived and produced by aero-engine pioneers Gustavus Green and R. J. Isaacson, were foremost in providing commendable alternative British power plants.

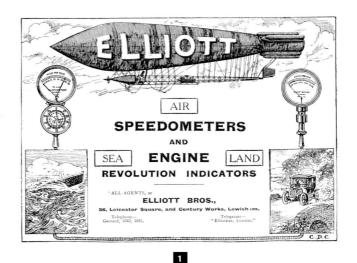

1

2

3

4

1 *Flight,* 2 January 1909.
2 *Flight,* 26 March 1910.
3 *Aero,* 19 October 1910.
4 *Aero,* 19 October 1910.
5 *Aero,* 26 August 1911.

The Isaacson 50 h.p. Engine in Flight on the Blackburn Monoplane.

Prices and particulars from—
THE ISAACSON RADIAL ENGINE Co., Ltd.,
BOYNE ENGINE WORKS, LEEDS.
Manufactured at the Works of—
MANNING, WARDLE & CO., LTD, BOYNE ENGINE WORKS, LEEDS.

5

THE CHIEF DIFFICULTY TO BE OVERCOME IN AVIATION IS THAT OF RENEWING SUPPLIES OF PETROL WHILE IN THE AIR

1

2

3

4

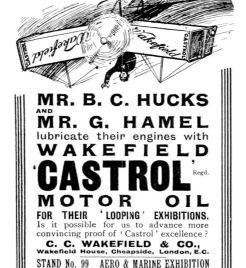

5

THE FUEL AND OIL COMPANIES

Alongside the airframe, engine and equipment makers, the fuel and oil suppliers soon began to associate themselves with the latest aviation achievements. Of particular interest here is the advertisement that appeared in the October 1909 edition of *Punch*, showing a far-sighted appreciation of air refuelling – and this just several weeks after Blériot made the first aerial crossing of the English Channel!

Note also the reference to Mr S.F. Cody who, by the time this advertisement for Vacuum Oil appeared in 1912, was invariably addressed as 'Colonel'.

1   *Punch,* 20 October 1909.
2   *Flight,* 1 December 1909.
3   London Aerodrome Official Programme, 1914.
4   *The Aeroplane,* 12 March 1914.
5   *Flight,* 7 September 1912.

THE GENERAL EQUIPMENT PROVIDERS

Among the multitude of specialised equipment suppliers now attending the industry, the Continental Tyre and Rubber Company was pre-eminent in providing the covering material for airships and aeroplanes.

On a more personal note, the Boddy Life-Saving Apparatus Company and the 'sporting tailors' Tautz and Company were just two of the clothing companies keen to meet the aviators' needs.

1

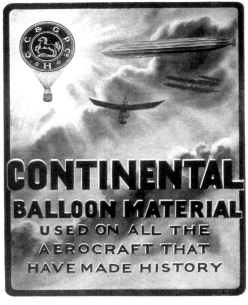

2

THE "BODDY"
LIFE SAVING JACKET

approved by the Board of Trade.

7 CERTIFICATES HAVE ALREADY BEEN GRANTED

A SIMILAR CERTIFICATE has been granted to each different pattern made. The jacket can not only be used as a life-saving device at sea but is also very useful and effective in the event of a rough landing on land. The front compartments of the jacket are also a protection to the chest and would act as a valuable buffer in the case of a bad landing throwing the pilot against the front of the machine. This point is worth noting, as a severe blow on the chest is likely to inflict grave internal injuries. The automatic action of the jacket makes it impossible for the wearer to get his or her head under water, even should the wearer be injured or become unconscious.

Just recently we have fitted out the Cunard Steamship, the Aquitania, with 3,260 life-saving Boddy Jackets; 2,415 jackets are now on order for the Cunard Steamship, Transsylvania. Orders are also in hand for the Canadian-Pacific Atlantic Steamship Lines, the Allan Line, the Nederland Steamship Company, in addition to many thousands supplied to the leading steamship companies.

A MODIFIED FORM OF THE BODDY JACKET IS NOW BEING MADE FOR THE USE OF INTENDING SWIMMERS AT THE SEA-SIDE

Illustrations of Lord Carbery and Mr. Brock wearing the Boddy Jacket specially made for pilots can be seen on pages 67 and 49.

Full particulars and Prices can be had on application to :—

THE BODDY LIFE - SAVING APPLIANCES (1914), LTD.
44 WILSON STREET, FINSBURY SQUARE, LONDON, E.C.

Telephone : London Wall 7650.   Telegrams : Subduing, Finsquare, London.

4

3

1   *Flight,* 28 August 1909.
2   *Flight,* 14 May 1910.
3   *The Aeroplane,* 14 June 1914.
4   *The Aeroplane,* 18 July 1914.

THE DARKENING SKIES, 1914–1918

Upon the declaration of war on 4 August 1914, Britain's first-line military aircraft strength amounted to 113 aeroplanes (including seaplanes) and six airships. This mixed assortment was fairly evenly divided between the Royal Flying Corps (RFC), formed in April 1912, and the Royal Naval Air Service (RNAS), formed in July 1914. However, when added to the 120 machines possessed by the French Air Service, the total almost equalled those held by Germany's armed forces.

The training of prospective service pilots was initially carried out at private schools, run primarily by the Bristol and Vickers companies, but these were mainly overtaken by the Central Flying School based at Upavon on Salisbury Plain and the Naval Wing's establishment at Eastchurch in Kent. Training soon became more advanced and by the time hostilities began, both service air arms possessed significant numbers of pilots whose natural abilities had already been finely tuned. There was, however, strong resistance among certain senior naval officers towards matters regarding 'the air'. Despite this, the Admiralty, now charged with the defence of the British Isles, sanctioned RNAS aircraft to attack the German Zeppelin hangars along the river Rhine and the airship factory itself on Lake Constance. In addition to troop-ship protection across the Channel, they engaged in long and exhaustive anti-submarine patrols in coastal waters throughout the war. In contrast to the antipathy initially encountered within the Admiralty, the Military Wing of the RFC was regarded from the outset as an integral part of the Army.

From its beginning in 1911 the training of military airmen made steady progress, with the early pre-war civilian training centres at Brooklands and Hendon later taken over by the RFC and RNAS. But by the outbreak of war instructional shortcomings were still leading to the deaths of too many young pilots, and a total lack of night-flying experience became a problem that had to be urgently addressed when German airships began to test the nation's defences under cover of darkness in May 1915. It became evident as the war progressed that not only was it necessary to seek continual improvement in the general level of piloting skills, but better quality aircraft were urgently required for home defence and to meet the new threat posed by the so-called 'Fokker Scourge'. This was the popular term for the new series of Eindeckers (monoplanes) employed by the Germans on the Western Front, which had a single Spandau machine gun capable of firing through the propeller arc. The main type to suffer at the hands of the agile Fokker was the slow, cumbersome and poorly armed B.E.2c, when undertaking reconnaissance patrols over the German lines. It was only following the introduction of the Nieuport Bébé scout and two machines, the Airco D.H.2 and the Royal Aircraft Factory F.E.2b, both designed by de Havilland, that in the spring of 1916 the imbalance in air fighting power was finally redressed. This was only achieved at a fearful cost, for the average life expectancy of an RFC aircrew member in the front line was now a mere eight weeks.

The training programme initiated by the RFC and maintained when it became the RAF on 1 April 1918 had been expanded to provide some 17,000 pilots in 1917 and 1918, together with supporting air and ground crews. In the latter half of the war, the Royal Aircraft Factory at Farnborough, along with other major companies such as Avro, Martinsyde, Sopwith, Vickers, Bristol, Blackburn, Armstrong Whitworth, The Aircraft Manufacturing Company and Shorts, now members of the newly formed Society of British Aircraft Constructors, produced a wide range and sizeable quantities of aircraft that, by 1918, enabled the Allies to gain a hard-won superiority over their German counterparts. In 1915, the Handley Page Co., in particular, had embarked upon the design and construction of a series of large bombing aircraft. The first of these, H.P.O/100, was a twin-engined biplane with a wing span of 100ft that met the requirement of the director of the Air Department, Commodore Murray F. Sueter, for a 'bloody paralyser of a bomber'! This was followed by the even more impressive H.P.0/400 and H.P.V/1500 machines which, along with de Havilland D.H.4., formed Britain's main aerial offensive force in the latter stages of the war.

Balloons and airships also provided an early indication of how airborne vehicles would give an extra dimension to warfare – indeed, they even went on to provide useful, if limited, service in the Second World War. It was, however, the aeroplane with its highly mobile destructive, transporting and observation capabilities that, in the 1914–18 conflict, changed military thinking forever.

The style of advertising employed during the war changed little from earlier years. Where possible, patriotic associations were now included, but, not unnaturally, it was the number of companies wanting to be identified with the war effort that made a noticeable impact on the public's aviation awareness.

THE FLYING SCHOOLS

Although the outbreak of war in 1914 soon saw the Bristol flying schools taken over by the military, others such as the Hall Flying School, the Beatty School of Flying, Pashley Bros and Hale on the south coast, and the Northern Aircraft School of Flying on Lake Windermere were typical of a number that continued to retain their private status.

1 *The Aeroplane*, 21 October 1914.
2 *Flight*, 30 April 1915.
3 *Flight*, 30 April 1915.
4 *Flight*, 23 June 1915.

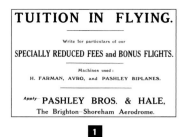

THE AIRFRAME CONSTRUCTORS

As the war progressed, several companies went from strength to strength. This is evident in the nature of their advertising, although the somewhat funereal nature of Avro's insert in an August 1914 edition of The Aeroplane might suggest that the publicity budget was running low! With the gathering pace of aircraft production, Mann Egerton and William Beardmore became typical of the many skilled and efficient sub-contracted firms that manufactured aircraft to the designs of other companies.

The Isle of Wight and Solent area continued to be at the centre of aircraft development and manufacture throughout the war with J. Samuel White, Saunders and Supermarine recognised as the pace-setting companies in seaplane and flying-boat design.

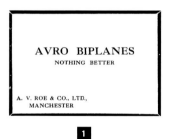

1 *The Aeroplane*, 12 August 1914.
2 *Flight*, 23 August 1916.
3 *Flight*, 31 May 1917.
4 *Flight*, 15 November 1917.
5 Source uncertain, *c*.1917.

1   *The Aeroplane,*
     18 November 1914.
2   *The Aeroplane,*
     2 December 1914.

THE FUEL AND OIL COMPANIES

Justifiably proud of its contribution to the war effort, the Shell Company made sure its products were directly associated with Britain's service achievements on land, sea and in the air.

1   *The Aeroplane,*
     15 November 1917.
2   *The Aeroplane,*
     26 August 1914.

THE GENERAL EQUIPMENT PROVIDERS

Contrasting examples of general equipment advertising are provided here by Thos. Firth, a major producer of armour plating materials, and the Calthrop Company. Both left little doubt as to the quality of their products, although it should be noted that parachutes were not introduced into general service use until after the war.

1   RAF recruiting poster, 1918.
2   WRAF recruiting poster,
     1918.

SERVICE RECRUITING

As the war moved into its final phase, the Royal Air Force (formed on 1 April 1918) and the Women's Royal Air Force invited Britain's youth to enlist. Such employment was, however, likely to be short-lived, for the end of hostilities soon brought massive reductions in the numbers of service personnel.

TOWARDS NEW HORIZONS, 1918–1939

The years between the two world wars saw several major mainstream developments take place in British aviation. Arguably the most significant was the realisation, shared with other nations, that air power would dictate the nature of warfare henceforth. Of equal importance, however, was the recognition that, after a faltering start but aided by several epic route-exploration flights by far-sighted pioneer Alan Cobham, a civil air transportation system could be set up that linked the United Kingdom not only with Europe, but also with the furthermost countries within its far-flung empire.

Another notable advancement was the establishment around the British Isles of many clubs and associations such as National Flying Services, which supplied not only excellent flying tuition but also a social network for the growing number of private pilots. In addition, these organisations provided many able contestants for the King's Cup and other prestigious air races promoted by the Royal Aero Club. Yet whilst these elements of civil flying began to gather strength, military aviation was experiencing problems, for the Royal Air Force's desire to remain an independent service had, early in the 1920s, become a much-debated topic within political circles. Fortunately, the persuasive case put forward by Air Marshal Sir Hugh Trenchard, then Chief of the Air Staff, finally won the day. He reasoned that, although not then required to prepare for an immediate war in Europe, the ability of the RAF to patrol and control dangerous trouble spots, such as India's North-West Frontier, provided a far more cost-effective option than the garrisoning of large numbers of troops in such isolated mountainous regions.

Although unavoidable, the immediate post-war reduction in the RAF's manpower resulted in some 22,000 newly demobilised pilots, initially recruited from school or university and untrained for any other occupation, adding to the growing ranks of ex-servicemen now facing an uncertain future. With but a few embryonic airlines struggling to stay in business, the chances of continuing a career in post-war aviation appeared to many an ex-pilot, to be bleak indeed. Others, however, saw these trying times as offering a golden opportunity, and purchased military surplus two-seat training machines such as the Avro 504K from the Aircraft Disposal Company at Croydon. Following a quick conversion to accommodate an extra passenger or two, these machines used also by several major aircraft producers, including Avro, Handley Page and Vickers, were flown by some fifty or so individual pilots sited at towns around the British coast in 1919, to provide thousands of thrill seekers with their first flight. After a couple of summer seasons, however, the novelty of joy-riding subsided and most of these 'quick flip' operators had vanished, leaving behind a trail of crashed or damaged aircraft, usually accompanied by a sizeable debt. Nonetheless, a few outfits survived and thrived throughout the 1920s, most notably the Berkshire Aviation Company which, in 1919, toured as far north as Edinburgh (even giving joyrides on a freezing cold Christmas Day), Surrey Flying Services and the Cornwall Aviation Company. The pleasure flight business 'ticked over' until the early 1930s, when it experienced a sudden resurgence, invariably forming part of the new and immensely popular itinerant air displays, best exemplified by Sir Alan Cobham's National Aviation Day Display. More usually referred to as Cobham's 'Flying Circus', his tours extended across the United Kingdom (and South Africa) between 1932–1935, and were undoubtedly the best organised and attended, but several other touring outfits also enjoyed considerable success. All featured well-known, record-breaking pilots, highly skilled aerobatic performers, parachutists (then regarded as very daring individuals) and a host of novelty items. The joyrides, now back in considerable demand, consisted of either sedate circuits around the airfield or, for the more adventurous, hair-raising escapades in which passengers, who were not strapped in, took part in pylon racing or aerial twists and turns guaranteed to test the strongest nerve and stomach. It was therefore hardly surprising when, at the outset of the Second World War, those volunteering for aircrew duties were asked if they had flown previously, some 75 per cent proudly answered, 'Yes – with Cobham's Flying Circus!'

As part of its inter-war fight for survival, the Royal Air Force carried out a series of long-distance flights across Africa and to the Far East. In addition to providing valuable training, these ventures were aimed at proving the mother country's ability to support its colonial administration in times of trouble. It also formed what was to become the famed High Speed Flight which, while overseas in 1927 and at home in 1929 and 1931, permanently secured the Schneider Trophy for Great Britain. This success proved to be of monumental importance, for not only did the latest Rolls-Royce engine 'R' that powered Supermarine's 1931 winning S.6B machine point the way to the legendary Merlin, which was to be the most-produced and reliable British power plant in the Second World War – but Supermarine's R.J. Mitchell, whose previous design experience was largely confined to slow-paced flying-boats, went on to design the superlative Spitfire.

In the late 1930s, a combination of inspired private company initiatives, coupled with a new and appreciative service chiefs' understanding of changing air warfare requirements, finally made sufficient Hawker Hurricane and Supermarine Spitfire fighters available, along with fully trained pilots, to win the Battle of Britain. It should be added that successive RAF expansion schemes at this time set in motion what was eventually to become a massive aerodrome construction and heavy bomber production programme. This resulted in the delivery of the first modern British four-engined bomber, the Short Stirling, to the RAF in August 1940. Present-day aviation historians are, nevertheless, generally agreed that, in this pre-war interim period, far too much reliance was placed on the assumed future effectiveness of the light and medium bomber. This led to valuable production resources being wastefully allocated to the Fairey Battle and the (admittedly more successful) Bristol Blenheim, which, despite the gallantry of their crews, were hopelessly outclassed in the opening aerial campaigns of the war. Unfortunately, the RAF's operational shortfalls, only exposed later in the heat of battle, were certainly not self-evident at the pre-war displays at Hendon and elsewhere. At such events and the service Station Open Days held annually throughout the country in the 1930s, the public was invited to witness, first hand, the 'unstoppable might' of Britain's newest fighting force. Certainly, the set-piece attacks by antiquated biplanes on static wood-and-canvas targets always presented an impressive fiery finale to the bombing displays, but they hardly represented an approach that matched the new realities of air warfare already being demonstrated by German squadrons in the Spanish Civil War.

The public patriotic fervour that supported the RAF's High Speed Flight in the Schneider Cup Races also extended to the home-grown competitors in what was, and is still, regarded by many as the world's greatest air contest – the 1934 MacRobertson Air Race from England to Australia. Unsurprisingly, national support centred on James and Amy Mollison who, as individual pilots, had won repeated entries in the record books with their astonishing flights to and from Australia and South Africa. By this time their achievements were continually being challenged by other long-distance, record-breaking pilots such as The Hon. Mrs Victor Bruce, Beryl Markham, Jean Batten, Charles Scott, Tom Campbell Black, Charles Kingsford Smith and Alex Henshaw, but as the 1930s came to a close, the general public and the media were paying far less attention to record breakers and air race winners and more to the increasingly important and expanding role of the airlines.

In 1919, the Aircraft Transport and Travel Company began Britain's first regular air services from Hounslow to Paris and Amsterdam. Handley Page Transport was quick to follow, and by 1922 four British companies were, unsuccessfully as it turned out, vying with competition that was heavily subsidised by the French Government. This led to the British closing ranks and merging the four major companies into a newly formed, state-owned corporation, Imperial Airways. After consolidating its European route structure, the airline then set out to establish empire routes, mainly via Cairo to the Middle East and India. Later expansion linked Australia and South Africa by land and flying-boat, but it was not until 1939 that non-stop crossings of the Atlantic by Imperial's air-refuelled, mail-carrying Short C-class flying-boats brought Canada within reach. Transatlantic passenger-carrying flights by British airlines would not, however, become available until after the war.

Over the twenty-year period between the wars, great strides were undoubtedly made in civil aviation. Aircraft became far more reliable and comfortable, and a number of civic aerodromes, such as those at Croydon and Heston, were constructed throughout Britain which boasted facilities that, by the standards of the day, were considered to be excellent. Unfortunately, it had also become evident that the British commercial aircraft then being introduced were lagging behind contemporary models being produced in America by the Douglas, Boeing and Lockheed companies. There was, unfortunately, no quick overnight solution, and it was only after the intervening war period that design disparities were seriously addressed. The ups and downs experienced by British aviation in the 1920s and 1930s, therefore, left a great deal to be done before the aeroplane could be regarded as a popular and affordable means of weekend pleasure or a convenient way of travelling that was not restricted to the 'well to do'.

What must also be appreciated was the establishment of Britain's aero-engine manufacturers in the world's aviation market, for in the inter-war period Rolls-Royce, Bristol, Armstrong Siddeley and Blackburn produced power plants entirely competitive with products manufactured in Europe or the USA.

In this oft-claimed inter-war 'golden age', the expansion of flying into the commercial and private civil areas engendered an avalanche of first-class advertising artwork. Flying events, service recruiting, company products and airline promotions provided a veritable field-day for aviation artists, and *Flight*, *The Aeroplane* and *Popular Flying* magazines continued to be the leading showcases for this wide range of imaginative talent.

THE FLYING SCHOOLS

There was seemingly no shortage of ex-pilots willing to take up a post-war flying career. Their enthusiasm was, however, dampened by the lack of opportunities in commercial aviation. The newly founded airlines possessed few aircraft and it was estimated that for the 22,000 pilots leaving the service, no more than 100 civilian vacancies existed. Yet for those who could afford it, flying training was available at a number of centres, including Stag Lane near Hendon, which became home to the de Havilland School of Flying and the London Aeroplane Club in 1920. It was also the London training centre for Royal Air Force Reserve officers. In 1930, the de Havilland operation moved to Hatfield, whilst rival concerns continued to thrive at Brooklands and elsewhere, not least at Cambridge, where entrepreneur Arthur Marshall was busy expanding his motor and aeronautical interests.

1

2

3

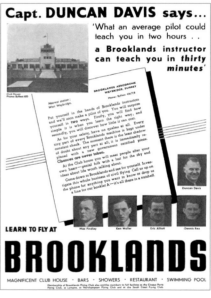

6

5

4

1   *Flight,* 28 August 1919.
2   *Flight,* 16 October 1919.
3   *Flight,* 23 October 1919.
4   *Flight,* 15 January 1920.
5   *The Aeroplane,* 9 October 1935.
6   *The Aeroplane,* 19 August 1936.

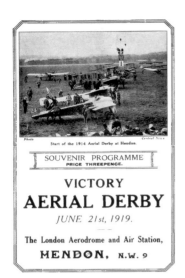

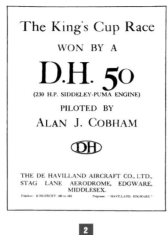

AIR RACES AND DISPLAYS

Keen to pick up where it left off in 1914, the London Aerodrome staged the 1919 Aerial Derby within weeks of the official resumption of civil flying in Britain on 1 May 1919. Surprisingly, perhaps, the programme's vintage illustration does little to reflect the advancements made in aircraft design and performance during the war.

The Royal Aero Club's King's Cup Air Race proved immensely popular during the inter-war period, as did the touring air displays led by well-known flyers such as Charles Barnard, Charles Scott and Tom Campbell Black. It was, however, Cobham's 'Flying Circus' which truly captured the public's imagination, giving over 1,000 performances throughout the United Kingdom between 1932 and 1935. Meanwhile, the Royal Air Force displays, held annually at Hendon, were showpiece exhibitions which, assisted by clever advertising, bolstered recruiting and convinced the taxpayer he was getting good value in service capability.

1   London Aerodrome programme, 1919.
2   *Flight*, 14 August 1924.
3   Aero Exhibition poster, 1929.
4   Touring display poster, 1930.
5   Touring display poster, 1931.
6   Royal Aero Club programme, Schneider Trophy, 1931.
7   National Aviation Day display poster, 1932.
8   *The Aeroplane*, 18 July 1934.
9   C.W.A. Scott's Flying Display programme, 1936.

7

8

9

10 RAF Display programme, 1921.
11 RAF Display programme, 1922.
12 RAF Display programme, 1923.
13 RAF Display programme, 1924.

14 RAF Display programme, 1925.
15 RAF Display programme, 1926.
16 RAF Display programme, 1927.
17 RAF Display programme, 1928.

18   RAF Display programme, 1929.
19   RAF Display programme, 1930.
20   RAF Display programme, 1931.
21   RAF Display programme, 1932.

22   RAF Display programme, 1933.
23   RAF Display programme, 1934.
24   RAF Display programme, 1935.
25   RAF Display programme, 1936.

26

27

1　　　　　　　　　　　　　　　**2**

THE PERSONAL TOUCH

The commercial astuteness of Frederick Handley Page was reflected in his involvement with the Aircraft Disposal Company. This was a firm created at Croydon in 1919 to handle the disposal of vast quantities of war surplus airframes, engines and accessories. 'H.P.' was begrudgingly admired by his business contemporaries for having emerged, via complicated legal manoeuvrings in both Britain and the USA, as the new company's agent with a very substantial profit.

1　*Flight,* 4 September 1919.
2　*Flight,* 13 May 1920.

THE AIRCRAFT CONSTRUCTORS

THE AIRCRAFT MANUFACTURING COMPANY LIMITED (AIRCO)

Following the end of the First World War, Airco, along with several other major aircraft manufacturers, faced diversification or closure. Whilst choosing to make car bodies, the company, chaired by George Holt Thomas, continued producing the Airco 16 (a civil conversion of the D.H.9A) and the Airco 18, designed from the outset as a commercial venture. In 1920, Airco formed an alliance with Birmingham Small Arms Limited (BSA), and shortly afterwards aircraft production ceased, with the assets and financial backing being transferred to form the de Havilland Aircraft Company Limited.

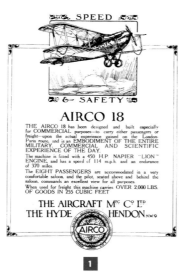

3   *The Aeroplane*, 1 July 1936.
1   *Flight*, 3 January 1920.
2   *The Aeroplane*, 18 July 1934.

AIRSPEED LIMITED

This was a company which arose in the wake of the cancellation of Britain's airship building programme in 1930. It provided the opportunity for key members of the newly expired Airship Guarantee Company, based at Howden in East Yorkshire, to set up their own company in nearby York. The company's name was allegedly suggested by the wife of designer Hessell Tiltman when it was decided that it should begin with 'A' to gain prominence in aviation directories and programmes etc.

Though producing several admirable designs throughout the 1930s, Airspeed struggled along with others to compete for orders with more familiar producers of light aircraft such as de Havilland and Blackburn.

1   *Flight*, 16 October 1919.
2   *Flight*, 1 January 1920.

THE ALLIANCE AEROPLANE COMPANY LIMITED

In the immediate post-war years, The Alliance Aeroplane Company Limited of Acton emerged as a company likely to make a significant impact on the commercial aircraft market. However, following the success of a record flight between London and Madrid, its future was fatally threatened when the P2 Seabird G-EAOX crashed on 13 November 1919 while attempting to become the first machine to fly from England to Australia.

THE A.V.ROE COMPANY LIMITED

Avro, having emerged from the First World War as a major constructor of training aircraft, including the 504 series, went on throughout the 1930s to produce a fine range of light aircraft. Most notable was the Avro Avian, favoured by the pioneering pilots 'Bert' Hinkler, Lady Heath and Bill Lancaster. The company's two-seat Tutor biplane became the RAF's standard trainer in the 1930s before production began to concentrate on the Avro 652 airliner for Imperial Airways and its military equivalent, the Anson patrol-bomber for the Royal Air Force, as advertised here.

1   *Flight*, 21 August 1919.
2   *Flight*, 11 January 1928.
3   *The Aeroplane*, 7 September 1938.

THE BRITISH AERIAL TRANSPORT COMPANY LIMITED

Struggling to achieve a toe-hold in post-war aviation, the British Aerial Transport Company secured the services of the talented Dutch designer, F. Koolhoven. He produced a series of good designs, but in the sterile commercial climate of the early 1920s, and despite its impassioned advertising, the company made little headway when competing against stronger companies such as Vickers, de Havilland and Bristol.

1   *Flight*, 21 August 1919.
2   *Flight*, 15 January 1920.

THE BLACKBURN AEROPLANE AND MOTOR COMPANY LIMITED

Along with its Lancastrian neighbour, A.V. Roe, the Yorkshire-based Blackburn company was the major northern contributor to British aviation development. Its inter-war range of designs extended from large flying-boats such as the Iris and Perth, to naval torpedo-attack and reconnaissance machines, such as Ripon, Baffin and Shark and, in the light aircraft field, the Bluebird trainer. By the outbreak of war, the Skua was equipping several Fleet Air Arm squadrons in the strangely combined fighter/dive-bomber role. Throughout this period, Blackburn and its chief rival, Fairey Aviation, were the primary suppliers of British naval aircraft, as suggested by the nautical flavour of their respective advertising campaigns.

The Blackburn Segrave Meteor, also advertised here, refers to one of several designs put forward to the firm by Sir Henry Segrave, who, in addition to his land speed racing credentials, was a member of the British Aviation Mission to Washington in 1918 and an ex-Royal Flying Corps fighter pilot.

Note also the introduction of the Botha, which, in competition with the Bristol Beaufort, was initially intended to equip Coastal Command with a twin-engined reconnaissance torpedo-bomber.

1

3

4

2

1   *The Aeroplane,* 12 January 1927.
2   *Flight,* 29 September 1927.
3   *Flight,* 22 May 1931.
4   *The Aeroplane,* 28 February 1934.

5   *The Aeroplane, c.1935.*
6   *The Aeroplane, c.1938.*
7   Empire Air Day programme, Boscombe
    Down, 1939.

5

6

7

1

2

THE BOULTON & PAUL COMPANY LIMITED

Though possessing in J.D. North a designer of undoubted talent, the company faced an uphill struggle to establish itself as a major supplier of first-rate aircraft. Achieving only limited success in the civil market, the firm found itself on a sounder footing with the delivery to the Royal Air Force of its Sidestrand and Overstrand bombers in the mid-1930s.

By this time, the company was seriously considering a four-gun turret fighter to meet the latest Air Ministry specification. Later named the Defiant, production was commenced in 1938, but the competition provided by the Spitfire and Hurricane soon rendered the turret-fighter concept obsolete.

1   *The Aeroplane,* 18 July 1934.
2   *The Aeroplane,* 26 April 1936.

THE BRISTOL AEROPLANE COMPANY LIMITED AND GEORGE PARNALL AND COMPANY

Building on the success achieved in the First World War, Bristol's airframe and engine designers went on to produce a wide range of machines for the home and overseas markets. Masterminding the Filton company's direction was Captain Frank S. Barnwell, who retained influential design positions from 1911 until his death in an air crash in August 1938. The use of Bristol aircraft by foreign air forces is reflected in the 'international' appeal of the company's inter-war advertising.

Although a founding member of the Society of British Aircraft Constructors, Bristol-based Parnall and Sons (aka George Parnall & Company and, from 1935, Parnall Aircraft Limited) attempted to enter the light aircraft market, with limited success. Several original designs were produced but the company relied largely on the manufacture of other types under licence throughout its existence.

1 *Flight*, 14 August 1924.
2 Source uncertain, *c*.1924.
3 Bristol Co. brochure, 1924.

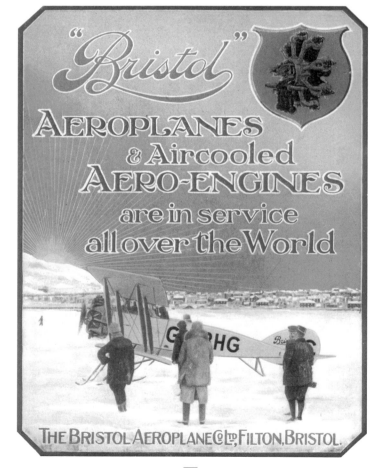

4 Bristol Co. brochure, c.1929.
5 Hendon Air Display programme, 1929.

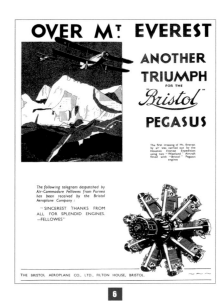

6 *Air and Airways, c.*1933.
7 *The Aeroplane,* 24 October 1934.
8 *The Aeroplane,* 29 April 1936.
9 *The Aeroplane,* 16 September 1936.
10 *The Aeroplane,* 1 September 1937.
11 *The Aeroplane,* 8 September 1937.

1

2

3

THE CIERVA AUTOGIRO COMPANY LIMITED

Never produced in large numbers for the light aircraft market, the autogiro nevertheless always attracted great public attention as a novelty feature at air displays. Differing from the helicopter in having a clutched free-wheeling (rather than engine driven) rotor, it was claimed that the autogiro was particularly easy to fly. It was, however, not unknown for dynamic instability to create excessive vibration with the machine on the ground, which resulted in a spectacular disintegration. Following the death of its inventor, Juan de la Cierva, in a fixed-wing aeroplane crash at Croydon in December 1936, the popularity of the autogiro waned, although several were used by the RAF at Old Sarum for radar calibration work in the early part of the Second World War.

4

1   *Flight*, 13 April 1933.
2   *The Aeroplane*, 18 July 1934.
3   *The Aeroplane*, 19 August 1936.
4   Source uncertain.

THE COMPER AIRCRAFT COMPANY LIMITED

Flight Lieutenant Nicholas Comper, having left the service in 1929, formed the Comper Aircraft Company at Hooton Park aerodrome near Liverpool. The first of the new company's products was the Swift which, when fitted with the 75h.p. Pobjoy R. engine, went on to achieve many national racing and long-distance flight successes. Comper's later designs failed to equal the popularity of the Swift, and it was this original type that ensured his name and reputation endured in later years.

1   *Flight*, 31 July 1931.

CUNLIFFE-OWEN LIMITED AND SCOTTISH AIRCRAFT AND ENGINEERING LIMITED

Both firms were wedded to producing licence-built variants of the American 'lifting fuselage' design conceived by Burnelli. Shown here is the advertisement for a bomber-transport, although a civil version, the Clyde Clipper, was also being proposed. Ahead of its time, for the 'lifting body' principle has subsequently been shown to be aerodynamically feasible, this futuristic design did not gain favour in British military or civil circles.

1   *The Aeroplane*,
2 December 1936.

THE DE HAVILLAND AIRCRAFT COMPANY LIMITED

De Havilland became an internationally renowned company following the success of its founder's military designs in the First World War, and the introduction, in 1925, of the Cirrus-powered Moth two-seat biplane. In addition to its design and manufacturing facilities, de Havilland also incorporated an Aeroplane Hire Service, with Alan Cobham as chief pilot. His long-distance, route-proving flights to India, South Africa and Australia in a D.H.50 provided a wonderful advertisement for the company, as did the achievements of other pilots such as Richard Bentley and Amy Johnson when flying de Havilland machines in their record-breaking ventures.

1   De Havilland Co. brochure, *c*.1923.
2   De Havilland Co. brochure, *c*.1926.

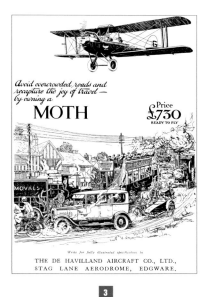

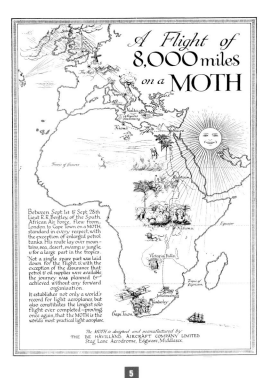

ENGLISH ELECTRIC AVIATION LIMITED

The English Electric company's early association with aviation lasted some eight years, from December 1918 until March 1926. During this time it concentrated its activities at Preston, having brought together three companies, Dick, Kerr and Company (of Preston), the Phoenix Dynamo Manufacturing Company Limited (Bradford) and the Coventry Ordnance Works, in 1918. As well as possessing a first-class design and manufacturing team, as the advertisement claims, the company also undertook the sub-contracted manufacture and assembly of Felixstowe F.3, F.5 and Fairey Atalanta flying-boats during the war years. After amalgamation into the English Electric organisation, only two types, the Ayr and the Kingston, emerged as original flying-boat designs. In parallel with these came the Wren motor-glider, which although possessed of remarkable economic performance, was only produced in very limited numbers before the aviation side was closed down. As is shown in chapter five, the company was later destined, post-1945, to re-appear at the cutting edge of aviation technology.

3 *The Aeroplane*, 4 May 1927.
4 De Havilland Co. brochure, c.1927.
5 *The Aeroplane*, 12 October 1927.
6 *Flight*, 23 November 1933.

1 *Flight*, 21 August 1919.

THE FAIREY AVIATION COMPANY LIMITED

Charles Richard Fairey was one of the handful of early aviation company founders who went on to see his firm prosper for half a century. Fairey aircraft (with those of Blackburn) were the backbone of British naval aviation throughout two world wars and the intervening period, and this is strongly reflected in the impressive art deco advertising that appeared in *Flight* and *The Aeroplane*. Other ventures into land-based machines for the Royal Air Force, notably the Hendon and Battle bombers, were not so successful (although some 2,200 examples of the latter were eventually produced). The major Fairey company locations were at Hayes, Stockport and Hamble, with Avions Fairey at Gosselies in Belgium created in the mid–1930s to assemble Fantôme fighters for the Belgian Air Force.

Clearly, the company placed great confidence in the skills of the artists Richard Trevithick and Leonard Bridgman, whose works dominate those presented here.

1   Source uncertain, *c.*1924.
2   Source uncertain, *c.*1925.
3   Source uncertain, *c.*1926.
4   Source uncertain, *c.*1927.
5   Source uncertain, *c.*1928.
6   Source uncertain, *c.*1929.

1

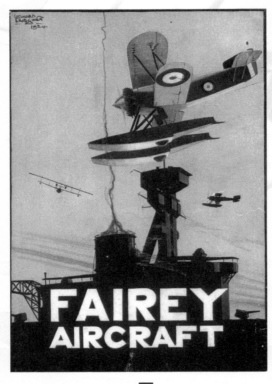

2

3

4

5

6

7 Source uncertain, *c.*1930.
8 *Flight,* 22 May 1931.
9 *The Aeroplane,* 13 February 1935.
10 Source uncertain, *c.*1935.

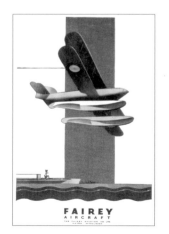

FAIREY AIRCRAFT

11

12

11 *The Aeroplane*, 5 February 1936.
12 *The Aeroplane*, 16 September 1936.

13   *Flight,* 10 June 1937.
14   *The Aeroplane,* 8 September 1937.
15   *The Aeroplane,* 7 September 1938.

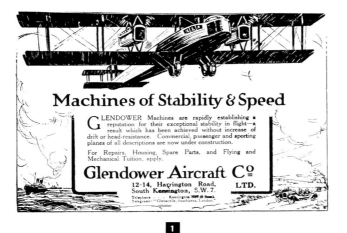

1 *Flight,* 23 October 1919.

THE GLENDOWER AIRCRAFT COMPANY LIMITED

Punching well above its weight in the post-war aviation world, the Glendower Company which had assembled D.H.4 and Sopwith Salamanders under sub-contract during the war soon fell by the wayside and folded in 1920.

1 Gloucestershire Aircraft Co. brochure, *c.*1923.

THE GLOUCESTERSHIRE AIRCRAFT/GLOSTER AIRCRAFT COMPANY LIMITED

Along with Bristol, Fairey, Blackburn and Vickers, the west country firms of, firstly, the Cheltenham-based Gloucestershire Aircraft and, later, Gloster at Cheltenham and Hucclecote were foremost in world-class aviation advertising.

Though largely in keeping with the times as a manufacturer of biplane fighters, Gloster did, when the occasion required it, allow the chief designer, H. P. Folland, and his team to produce a monoplane masterpiece. There was no better example than that of the Gloster VI seaplane racer in 1929. It was perhaps unfortunate for the company that, unlike its arch competitor, Vickers Supermarine, it did not pursue the logical line of monoplane fighter design with the vigour of R.J. Mitchell. However, the glamour of the company's advertising is evident in this selection of inter-war studies.

2

4

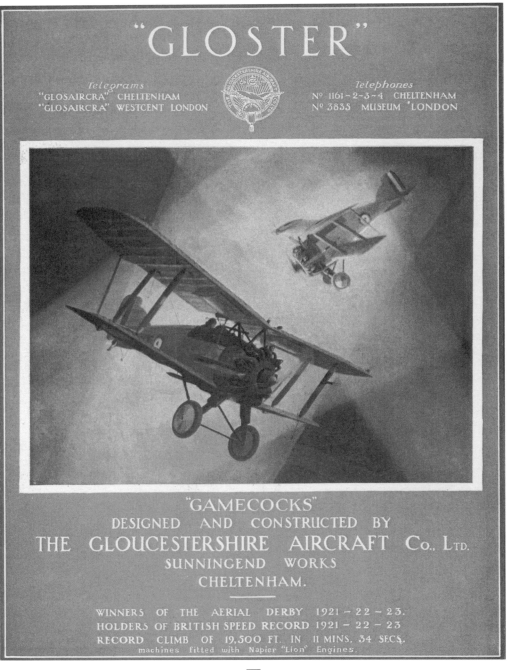

3

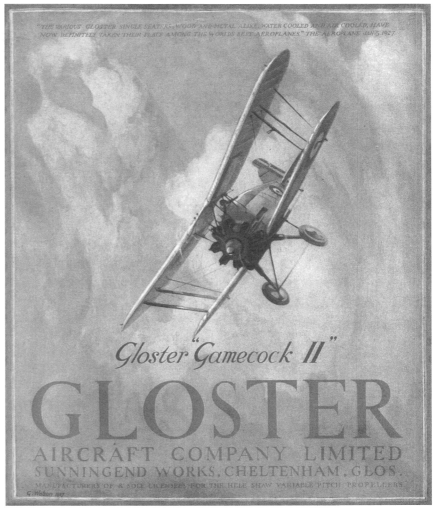

7

8

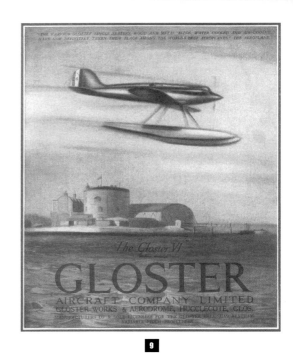

9

10

11

7 Gloster Aircraft Co. brochure, *c.*1928.
8 Gloster Aircraft Co. brochure, *c.*1928.
9 Gloster Aircraft Co. brochure, *c.*1930.
10 *The Aeroplane*, 5 February 1936.
11 Gloster Aircraft Co. brochure, *c.*1936.

12 Gloster Aircraft Co. brochure, c.1937.

THE HANDLEY PAGE COMPANY LIMITED

Surprisingly, the Handley Page Company was not so well represented in the trade press as other equally well-known companies. This may well reflect a view held at board level that the company's reputation and its products were entirely self-sufficient. However, examples of Handley Page's occasional exploration into the world of advertising are captured here, firstly with its 1920 promotion of the W.8 airliner and, in the late 1930s, the Hampden bomber.

1   *Flight*, 8 January 1920.
2   *Flight*, 9 September 1937.
3   Source uncertain, *c.*1938.

THE WORLD'S MOST LUXURIOUS COMMERCIAL AEROPLANE.

HANDLEY PAGE TYPE W.8,
FITTED WITH 2-450 h.p. NAPIER ENGINES.

HANDLEY PAGE L^{TD.} LONDON, ENGLAND.

2

1

3

F. HILLS AND SONS

With so many of the British aircraft producers engaged on military contracts, a large number of the light aircraft supplied to the flying clubs in the late 1930s were of foreign origin. Although American companies, such as Aeronca, Piper and Taylorcraft, were pre-eminent, Manchester-based F. Hills and Sons also undertook the manufacture under licence of the Czechoslovakian Praga Air Baby for the training market. Although this machine failed to appeal to private owners, it was widely used by, among others, the Whitney Straight chain of flying clubs in southern England.

MARTINSYDE LIMITED

Although another founder company within the Society of British Aircraft Constructors, Martinsyde, along with several other notable wartime companies, did not survive the post-war contraction of the industry. This advertisement, based on the success of the F4 fighter, heralded the swansong of the firm.

1 C.W.A. Scott Air Display programme, 1935.

1 *Flight,* 21 August 1919.

NIEUPORT AND GENERAL AIRCRAFT COMPANY LIMITED

Although Nieuport companies were founded in 1916 by Sir Samuel Waring (of Waring and Gillow, the famed furniture manufacturers), it was not until immediately after the war that the title British Nieuport and General Aircraft Company was finally adopted. Despite the confidence expressed in this series of imaginative *Flight* advertisements in 1919, the company faded away in the early 1920s, and its chief designer, H.P. Folland, moved on to join the Gloucestershire Aircraft Company.

1 *Flight*, 21 August 1919.
2 *Flight*, 4 September 1919.
3 *Flight*, 16 October 1919.
4 *Flight*, 23 October 1919.
5 *Flight*, 13 May 1920.

1

2

3

THE WAR GOD'S GIFT TO PEACE

BRITISH
NIEUPORT
& GENERAL AIRCRAFT Co Ltd

Telephone:
WILLESDEN 2455.
(3 lines)

CRICKLEWOOD,
LONDON, N.W.2.

Telegrams:
"NIEUSCOUT.
CRICKLE. LONDON."

On the left is illustrated the Nieuport Night Hawk fighting scout.
On the right is the special civilian two-seater machine.

4

A Pointer
to
Progress

The first post-war
commercial flights
in India have been
performed by the famous
NIEUPORT "NIGHTHAWK."
Complete success was
a foregone conclusion—
verb. sap.

BRITISH
NIEUPORT
& GENERAL AIRCRAFT Co Ltd

Telegrams:
"Nieuscout, Crickle, London."

CRICKLEWOOD, LONDON, N.W. 11.

Telephone:
Willesden 2455 (3 line

5

PERCIVAL AIRCRAFT COMPANY, PHILLIPS AND POWIS AIRCRAFT (MILES), BRITISH KLEMM AEROPLANE COMPANY LIMITED

These advertisements form a general grouping of the British light aircraft producers that most influenced the private owner and racing fraternities in the 1930s.

Note: Separate attention has been given to Avro, de Havilland and Blackburn which were, arguably, in a somewhat 'higher league' in terms of manufacturing capability and worldwide sales.

The relationship between Phillips and Powis and Miles Aircraft has proved confusing to many a casual observer (certainly the author). Suffice it to say here, that whilst Phillips and Powis Aircraft Limited managed the Reading aerodrome and associated flying club, the aircraft they produced always carried the prefix 'Miles'. Miles Aircraft Limited was later formally created in 1943, having by then bought out Phillips and Powis!

1

2

1   *The Aeroplane,* 18 July 1934.
2   *The Aeroplane,* 25 July 1934.
3   *The Aeroplane,* 18 December 1934.
4   *The Aeroplane,* 19 October 1935.
5   *The Aircraft Engineer,* 29 April 1937.
6   *The Aeroplane,* 8 September 1937.
7   *Flight,* c.1939.

3

4

5

7

6

THE SAUNDERS, SARO AND SPARTAN COMPANIES

Between 1908 and 1928, S.E. Saunders Limited was engaged in boat-building, sub-contracted aircraft assembly and the design and manufacture of several machines to its own design.

Following the injection of new capital into the firm and the succeeding of Sam Saunders by Sir Alliott Verdon Roe in 1928, the company was restructured to become Saunders-Roe Limited, usually abbreviated to SARO. Although the company's later style of advertising, as typified here, is certainly eye-catching, the attached caption seems distinctly low-key and understated.

Also based on the Isle of Wight, the Spartan Aircraft Company co-existed alongside SARO, until it was absorbed into the bigger firm in early 1933. Although aircraft were still produced bearing the Spartan name, by 1935 even this had disappeared.

2

1

Adaptability

● *Five Paying Passengers* ; *265 lbs. Luggage* : *620 Miles*

● *Seven Paying Passengers* ; *390 lbs. Luggage* : *310 Miles*

PLUS pilot, wireless-operator-mechanic, metal airscrews, wireless set and toilet facilities

and Performance

● Recently a Spartan Cruiser completed a return flight over three continents, Europe-Africa-Asia, a total distance of 21,900 miles.

● This journey is the longest Czechoslovakian flight yet made and comes as a fitting follow-on to the England-Australia-England flight of last year. The 000 miles then covered still constitute the longest vate charter flight on record.

SPARTAN CRUISER
THREE-ENGINED CABIN MONOPLANE
SPARTAN AIRCRAFT LTD., COWES, ISLE OF WIGHT

3

1 *Flight*, 28 August 1919.
2 *Flight*, 13 April 1933.
3 *The Aeroplane*, 24 October 1934.
4 *Flight*, 9 September 1937.

Flight, September 9, 1937. Supplement vii

SARO "LONDONS" OVER GIBRALTAR returning to England on a non-stop flight upon the completion of co-operation exercises with the Fleet

4

SHORT BROS LTD

By 1920, having also pioneered the use of stressed metal skin in manufacture, Shorts was well established as a leading aviation company. The firm then concentrated mainly on producing flying-boats and float-planes, with an occasional departure into land-plane designs such as the Short Scylla and Scion airliners and, in the late 1930s, the Stirling heavy bomber. Note that the metal floats fitted to the Valetta were 40ft in length – the largest ever built! The company's reputation was further enhanced when Imperial Airways placed an unprecedented order for twenty-eight machines which were soon referred to as the 'C Class' flying-boats. These featured strongly in the airline's advertising in the late 1930s.

ALL-METAL AEROPLANES SEAPLANES & FLYING-BOATS.

SHORT (ROCHESTER BROS. & BEDFORD) LTD. WHITEHALL HOUSE. 29-30, CHARING CROSS. LONDON, S.W.1.

2

SHORT BROS.
(ROCHESTER & BEDFORD), LTD.
SEAPLANE WORKS, ROCHESTER, KENT.

FIRST IN 1911
STILL AHEAD IN 1922.

The "CROMARTY," the largest Seaplane afloat.—*Evening News, 30-8-22.*

1911
The First British Twin-Float Seaplane.

1920
The First British All-Metal Aeroplane.

1922
The Largest British Flying-Boat to be success-fully flown.

London Office:
Phone: Regent 278.   **WHITEHALL HOUSE, 29-30, CHARING CROSS, S.W.1.**   Grams: Tested, Phone, London.

1

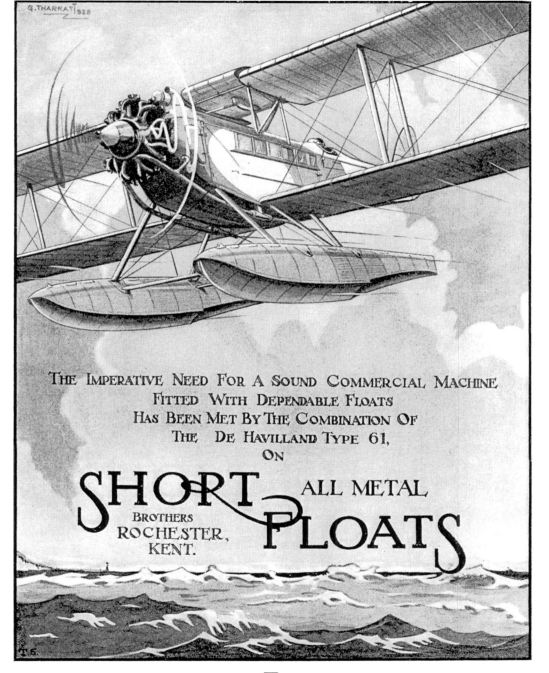

1   *Aeronautical Engineering,* 1 November 1922.
2   *The Aeroplane,* 14 January 1925.
3   *The Aeroplane,* 13 January 1926.
4   Short Bros brochure, *c.*1928.

5

6

7

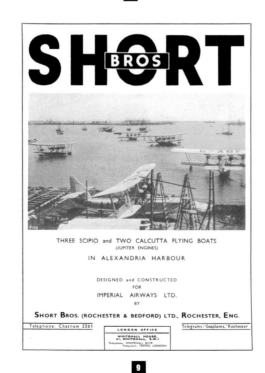

8

9

5   *The Aeroplane*, 15 May 1929.
6   *The Aeroplane*, 4 November 1931.
7   *The Aeroplane*, 12 July 1933.
8   *Flight*, 28 August 1919.
9   *The Aeroplane*, 25 July 1934.
10   *The Aeroplane*, 5 February 1936.
11   *The Aeroplane*, 8 September 1937.
12   *The Aeroplane*, 13 April 1938.
13   *Flight*, 13 July 1939.

SHORT SINGAPORE
fitted with Rolls-Royce engines

SHORT BROS (ROCHESTER & BEDFORD) LTD. ROCHESTER. ENG

10

ONE OF THE NEW EMPIRE FLYING BOATS
Constructed for
IMPERIAL AIRWAYS
by
SHORT BROS. (ROCHESTER & BEDFORD) LTD.
ROCHESTER, ENGLAND

11

SHORT BROS. (ROCHESTER & BEDFORD) LTD. ROCHESTER

12

SHORT SUNDERLANDS
Designed and Built
by
SHORT BROS.
of
ROCHESTER

13

THE SOPWITH AND HAWKER COMPANIES

The Sopwith Aviation and Engineering Company Limited was an undoubted stalwart of the country's industrial war effort; the production figures shown in this 1919 edition of *Flight* speak for themselves. However, the drastic curtailment of orders that followed the end of the war saw the company diversify into the production of car bodies and motor cycles. By 1920, the firm, faced with Excess War Profits Duty, was forced into insolvency but the Sopwith legacy was cleverly transferred to one of its principal founders, Harry Hawker. Accordingly, a new company, H.G. Hawker Engineering Company Limited, was announced with a board of directors virtually identical to that of Sopwith. Sadly, Hawker failed to see the growth of his company into a world-class organisation. Though already terminally ill with tubercular disease of the spine, he was killed on 12 July 1921 when flying a Nieuport Goshawk in preparation for the Aerial Derby. The Hawker name, however, was destined to remain in the forefront of British aviation, until it was finally absorbed into British Aerospace in 1977.

1 *Flight*, February 1919.
2 *Flight*, 8 January 1920.
3 Hawker Co. brochure, *c.*1923.

4 *The Aeroplane*, 5 February 1936.
5 *The Aeroplane*, 29 June 1938.
6 *The Aeroplane*, 23 November 1938.

THE REDWING AIRCRAFT COMPANY LIMITED

Just eighteen months after its incorporation on 12 August 1929, the Robinson Aircraft Company Limited changed its name to Redwing Aircraft Company Limited. Though never seriously challenging the popularity of the Moth, Avian or Bluebird, the Redwing biplane was judged to possess excellent slow-speed handling, a very short take-off run and good climb performance. Redwing's activities were mainly based at Croydon, but a flying school was also set up at Gatwick.

1 *Flight,* 22 May 1931.

THE VICKERS AND SUPERMARINE COMPANIES

As a result of the complex merging of firms within the industry, changes in company titles could often prove perplexing. An examination of this group of first-class advertisements certainly calls for some flexibility of interpretation – especially where the integration of Supermarine into the Vickers organisation is concerned. Nevertheless, the diversity of products, ranging from Vimy to Spitfire, reflects the in-depth strength and brilliance of the design teams resident at Weybridge and Southampton in the inter-war years, and it should be noted that these were just some of the types they produced!

1 *Flight,* 21 August 1919.
2 *Flight,* 16 October 1919.

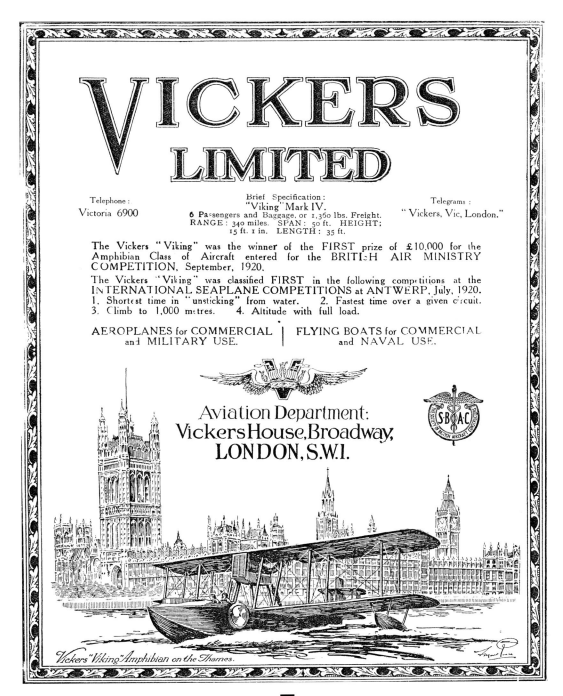

3 *Aeronautical Engineering,*
1 November 1922.

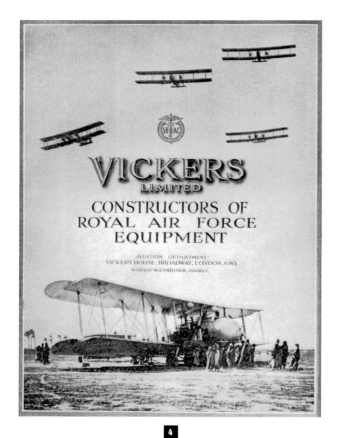

4 Source uncertain, *c.*1923.
5 Source uncertain, *c.*1926.

6 Source uncertain, *c*.1927.
7 Source uncertain, *c*.1928.

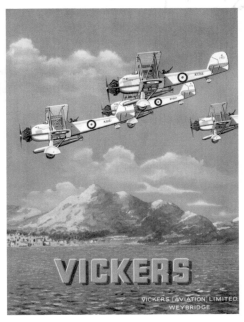

9 Royal Aero Club programme, 1931.
10 RAF Display programme, 1933.
11 *The Aeroplane*, 25 July 1934.
12 RAF Display programme, 1935.
13 RAF Display programme, 1935.

14   RAF Display programme, 1934.

"Spitfire I"

THE SUPERMARINE AVIATION WORKS (VICKERS) LIMITED

15

"Wellesley"

VICKERS (AVIATION) LIMITED

16

15 RAF Display programme, 1936.
16 RAF Display programme, 1937.

THE WESTLAND AIRCRAFT WORKS

The Westland Aircraft Works at Yeovil (a branch of Petters Limited) was a founding member of the Society of British Aircraft Constructors. It soon became a major sub-contractor, assembling Short Bros, de Havilland and Vickers machines throughout the war and production of the D.H.9A continued well into the post-war years.

The Westland Limousine, advertised here, won the 1920 Air Ministry competition for transport aeroplanes but commercial orders were not forthcoming. Work in the Twenties and Thirties continued to revolve around sub-contracting but a number of the company's own designs such as the Wapiti, Widgeon and Wessex went on to make a successful impact on the civil market. By 1938, the Lysander and Hawker Hector, the latter built under sub-contract, were the main types (both destined for Army co-operation) coming off the production line.

1

2

3

1   *The Aeroplane,*
    13 February 1918.
2   *The Aeroplane,*
    13 February 1918.
3   *Flight*, 28 August 1919.
4   *The Aeroplane*, 25 May
    1932.
5   *Flight*, 13 April 1933.

4

5

WILLIAM BEARDMORE AND COMPANY LIMITED

The Beardmore Company made a highly significant contribution to aircraft and aero-engine production in the First World War. However, after suffering the pangs of post-war contraction, the firm closed its aviation department in 1921, only to re-open it in 1924. Products designed and constructed at Dalmuir in Scotland ranged in size from the Wee Bee, winner of the 1924 Light Aeroplane Competition, to the massive, 157ft-span Inflexible monoplane. Having experienced limited success throughout the 1920s, Beardmore withdrew from aircraft manufacture in 1930.

1

1   *Flight*, 16 October 1924.

THE FUEL AND OIL COMPANIES

Relatively few oil and fuel suppliers were involved with the aviation industry, so their promotional styles have been combined in this grouping. Of special interest is the advent of sky-writing, pioneered by Major Jack Savage, which proved to be a popular and clever form of advertising in the inter–war years.

Not surprisingly, the leading aviation personalities of the period were obliged to recognise their sponsors' products, though not perhaps in the overt style of today's 'celebrities'.

1   Source uncertain, *c.*1922.
2   *The Aeroplane*, 29 February 1928.
3   *Flight*, 22 May 1931.
4   Scheider Trophy programme, 1931.
5   *Air and Airways*, *c.*1933.

6 Source uncertain, *c.*1933.
7 *Air and Airways, c.*1933.
8 *The Aeroplane,* 28 February 1934.
9 *The Aeroplane,* 29 April 1936.
10 *Popular Flying,* April 1938.
11 Source uncertain, *c.*1938.

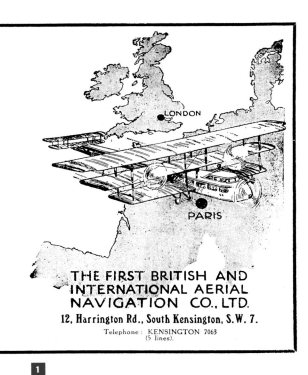

The Pioneer Passenger Line.

The First British and International Aerial Navigation Company has been formed with the object of inaugurating daily passenger services to and fro between England, France, Ireland and other countries. Bases have already been secured and the designs of the machines approved, so that no time will be lost in making an accomplished fact of the Pioneer Passenger Air Service. Those interested are advised to write for full particulars, and the Company will, on request, keep correspondents posted with each fresh development and each step of progress.

THE FIRST BRITISH AND INTERNATIONAL AERIAL NAVIGATION CO., LTD.
12, Harrington Rd., South Kensington, S.W. 7.
Telephone : KENSINGTON 7063 (5 lines).

1

2

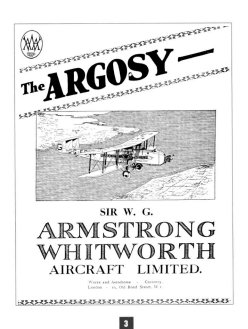

3

THE AIRLINES

Airline advertising in the 1920s and 1930s represented, without any doubt, the touchstone of public appeal. Designed to capture the patronage of the relative few who could afford to travel in luxurious style, the posters commissioned by Imperial Airways were highly seductive, and today command very high prices at the auction houses.

The airlines' early advertising just after the First World War was, naturally, not too ambitious, but the growing strength of Imperial, and other national airlines, can be gauged from the illustrations gradually moving to full colour, some of the most appealing being included here. By late 1939, Imperial Airways and British Airways had merged to form British Overseas Airways Corporation, and the so-called 'golden era' had passed.

Note: Although the Argosy advertisements are directly promoting the Armstrong Whitworth Company, their airline association makes it equally appropriate to include them in this section.

1   *Flight*, 9 January 1919.
2   *Airways*, August 1926.
3   *The Aeroplane*, 31 August 1927.

FOLLOW THE SWALLOW

THE Armstrong Whitworth Silver Wing Argosy Air Liner has been selected by Imperial Airways, Limited, as the most suitable machine for their First Winter Air Cruise over Northern Africa and the South-West of Europe.

The Silver Wing Argosy, with its three 385-425 h.p. air-cooled Armstrong Siddeley Jaguar engines, has already proved its absolute reliability, great economy of running and ease of maintenance, on the London-Paris airway.

The First Winter Five Weeks' Air Cruise marks another advance in commercial aviation, and the fact that an Armstrong Whitworth aeroplane fitted with Armstrong Siddeley engines has been selected for the task proves that the Silver Wing Argosy Air Liner is the safest and most luxurious aircraft in the world.

Sir W. G.

ARMSTRONG WHITWORTH

AIRCRAFT LIMITED,

Works & Aerodrome: Coventry.
London : 10, Old Bond St., W.1.

4

6

4   *The Aeroplane*, 7 December 1927.
5   Imperial Airways poster, 1930.
6   Source uncertain, *c*.1932.
7   Airline poster, *c*.1932.
8   Airline poster, *c*.1932.
9   *Bystander* magazine, *c*.1933.

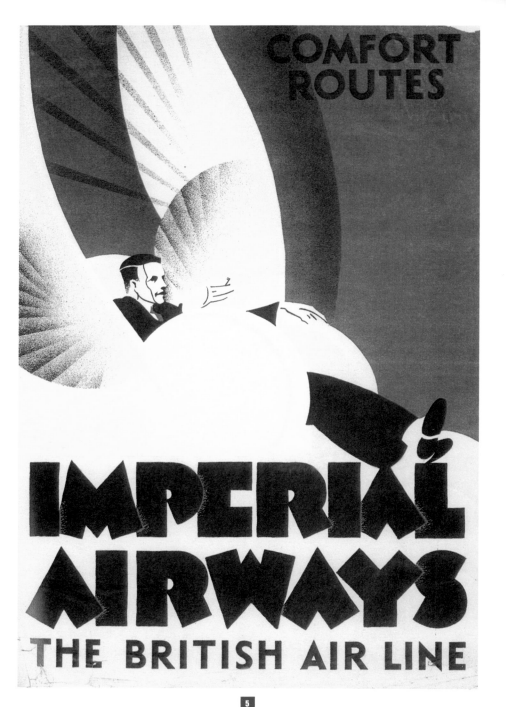

5

9

7

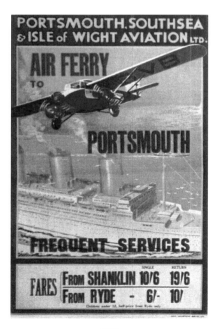

8

10

11

13

12

10 Source unknown, *c*.1934.
11 Imperial Airways poster, 1935.
12 Imperial Airways poster, 1935.
13 Airline poster, *c*.1935.
14 *Air and Airways*, *c*.1936.
15 Imperial Airways poster, 1936.
16 Imperial Airways poster,
     c.1936.
17 Imperial Airways poster, 1936.

20

BRITISH AIRWAYS

22

18 Imperial Airways poster, 1937.
19 Imperial Airways poster, 1937.
20 Imperial Airways poster, 1937.
21 *The Aeroplane*, 21 April 1937.
22 *The Aeroplane*, 23 June 1938

21

THE ENGINE MAKERS

This grouping pulls together the notable companies that powered British machines in the inter-war period. It is appropriate to include here one or two major engine accessory suppliers, such as the airscrew and sparking plug manufacturers, because, it might be conceded, the more evident end product would not have got far without them! The advertisements represent an age when individual companies fought for survival in a very tough post-war market. Orders were slim and inevitably some firms, Beardmore and Sunbeam being good examples, simply could not compete. Bristol, Armstrong Siddeley, Rolls-Royce, de Havilland and Napier proved to be survivors at this stage but, as will be shown later, even these strong companies would eventually be forced to amalgamate.

1

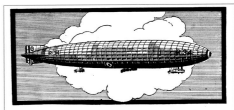

2

1 *Flight*, 21 August 1919.
2 *Flight*, 21 August 1919.
3 Napier Co. brochure, *c*.1920.
4 *The Aeroplane*, 31 July 1931.
5 *The Aeroplane*, 10 January 1936.
6 *The Aeroplane*, 28 February 1934.
7 *The Aeroplane*, 18 July 1934.
8 *The Aeroplane*, 10 July 1935.
9 *The Aeroplane*, 5 February 1936.
10 *The Aeroplane*, 1 April 1936.

3

4

5

6

7

9

10

GIPSY

THE NEAREST THING IN ENGINES TO IMMORTALITY

8

11

12

13

14

15

16

17

18

THE GENERAL EQUIPMENT SUPPLIERS

This assortment of advertisements, best described as 'general', represents the companies that clearly provided essential services to the aviation industry. From furniture to flying suits, fabrics to finishes, and materials to machine guns, this short miscellany still covers a wide range of supporting firms. Clearly, comfort is the keyword where seating is concerned, according to the Bowser advertisement in a July 1919 edition of *The Aeroplane*. Added to this, 'only the best is good enough for our flying men' is the message from Burberrys and Dunhills in 1919. Jack Alcock's comment that no rubber or cement is used in the Carapace Air-Suit's waterproofing invites amusing speculation, whilst many others, Helliwells especially, continued to provide industrial inspiration!

1　*The Aeroplane*, July 1919.
2　*Flight*, 10 July 1919.
3　Source uncertain, *c*.1919.
4　*Flight*, 25 September 1919.
5　*Flight*, 9 October 1919.
6　*Flight*, 29 September 1927.
7　*Flight*, 17 April 1931.
8　*Flight*, 17 April 1931.
9　RAF Display programme, *c*.1932.
10　*The Aeroplane*, 30 August 1933.
11　*Flight*, 26 April 1934.
12　*The Aeroplane*, 18 July 1934.

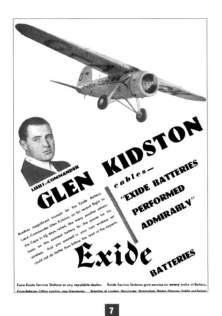

LIEUT.-COMMANDER GLEN KIDSTON *cables —* "EXIDE BATTERIES PERFORMED ADMIRABLY"

Exide BATTERIES

From Exide Service Stations or any reputable dealer. Exide Service Stations give service on **every** make of Battery.

7

HULL OFFERS —
to AIRCRAFT CONSTRUCTORS *and* ALLIED INDUSTRIES

100 ACRES AVAILABLE FOR AIRCRAFT CONSTRUCTION & ALLIED INDUSTRIES

The Hull Corporation will afford every encouragement to Aircraft Constructors and Allied Trades to establish their Works on the Attractive and Spacious Site adjoining the Aerodrome. **Apply** THE TOWN CLERK, GUILDHALL, HULL.

8

The pilot sat unharmed in the cockpit throughout the blaze — both being protected with **Bestobell Products**

This demonstration was given at the Royal Aeronautical Society's Garden Party on Sunday, May 5th, by **BELL'S ASBESTOS & ENGINEERING SUPPLIES LIMITED, SLOUGH**

("BESTOBELL" is the Registered Trade Mark of Bell's Asbestos and Engineering Supplies Ltd.)

9

PALMER CORD AERO TYRE

PALMER AIRCRAFT LANDING WHEELS TYRES AND BRAKES

10

The Short 'Scylla' (four Bristol "Jupiter")

With their long experience of aircraft manufacture, particularly for the arduous conditions of marine service, it is only natural that Messrs. Short Brothers should rely upon Cellon, the Dope of Proved Efficiency. The new Short 'Scylla' pictured above, with its wing span of 113 feet and main plane area of 2,615 square feet, is doped with Cellon Scheme X.

CELLON
THE DOPE OF PROVED EFFICIENCY

Cerric Lacquers comply with D.T.D. Specifications for metal parts, cockpits, propellers. Particulars on application.

CELLON LTD., Richmond Road, KINGSTON-ON-THAMES
(Contractors to H.M. and Foreign Governments).

11

"SEEMS LIKE THAT LITTLE FIELD NEAR LONDON IS GETTING BIGGER!"

AND A BIGGER AIRPORT IS A BETTER AIRPORT
Permanent traffic control and a 57% increase in landing area mark the second stage of Heston development. There is plenty of room for further expansion.

AIRWORK LIMITED
HESTON AIRPORT
New Telephone Number · · · HOUnslow 2345.
And at Bristol and Manchester.

12

13

THE THREE DE HAVILLAND COMETS
IN THE
ENGLAND—AUSTRALIA RACE
WERE COATED WITH
TITANINE
"SATIN FINISH"

TITANINE-EMAILLITE LTD., HEAD OFFICE AND WORKS: COLINDALE, LONDON, N.W.9

THE
ARMSTRONG WHITWORTH
AW.XXIII
TRANSPORT BOMBER

DOPED WITH
TITANINE
THE WORLD'S PREMIER
DOPE

TITANINE - EMAILLITE LTD. HEAD OFFICE AND WORKS COLINDALE, LONDON, N.W.9

14

Mrs MARKHAM GETS THROUGH
in her
PERCIVAL VEGA GULL (Gipsy VI. Engine)
having relied on
SMITH'S INSTRUMENTS
and
HUSUN P.4.COMPASS
in her brilliant Solo Flight
across the Atlantic

SMITH'S AIRCRAFT INSTRUMENTS
CRICKLEWOOD WORKS
LONDON N.W.2

15

1913   1936
STREAMLINE
and always
PALMER
LANDING EQUIPMENT

16

13 *The Aeroplane,* 14 November 1934.
14 *The Aeroplane,* 29 January 1936.
15 *The Aeroplane,* 16 September 1936.
16 *The Aeroplane,* 25 March 1936.
17 *The Aeroplane,* 21 April 1937.
18 *Flight,* 29 April 1937.
19 *The Aeroplane,* 16 June 1937.
20 *The Aeroplane,* 27 April 1938.
21 *The Aeroplane,* 4 May 1938.

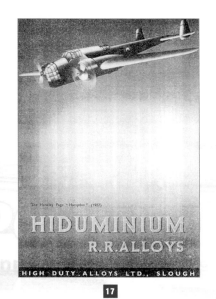

17

18

19

20

21

22 *Popular Flying,* April 1938.
23 *Flight,* 6 July 1939.
24 *The Aeroplane,* 7 September 1938.
25 Lockheed Company brochure, 1939.

4

THE BREAKING STORM, 1939–1945

The succession of German territorial gains in Europe, which culminated in Hitler's attack on Poland in September 1939, inevitably brought Britain into conflict with Germany. The final declaration of war, however, had fortunately been preceded by a warning period which allowed the RAF to reassess its capabilities and, crucially, to obtain more fighter squadrons for home defence. This meant that despite having to fight draining rearguard actions in France and Norway, Fighter Command was just able to muster sufficient aircraft and pilots to meet, and eventually beat, the Luftwaffe's bomber fleets in the Battle of Britain. The RAF's first few probing sorties over the German coastal ports quickly confirmed that its inadequately armed twin-engined bomber force would be unable to mount daytime operations without unacceptable losses. It was not until mid-1942 that Bomber Command, then being re-equipped with greatly improved aircraft such as the Lancaster, Halifax and Mosquito, was able to make a serious impact on the German war effort. At this time, RAF fighter squadrons were also engaged in offensive sweeps over France and in the valiant defence of Malta, while in 1943 growing Allied war activities throughout the North African, Sicilian and Italian war theatres were carried out under a new Mediterranean Air Command.

Also in 1943 two committees were formed whose findings would significantly affect the future of British aviation. The first of these involved US and British officials deciding the types of warplane each country should concentrate on producing. The outcome of this resulted in the manufacture of transport aircraft largely residing in America, and British industry focussing on the supply of fighters and bombers. This conclusion was destined to place Britain at a long-term disadvantage, for when the war ended the Americans were able to call upon machines such as the Dakota, Skymaster and Constellation that had amassed considerable operational hours on Far Eastern long-haul supply routes. British airlines could only draw upon the Avro York and the Lancastrian, Halton and Viking airliner adaptations of the Lancaster, Halifax and Wellington bombers.

The second committee, chaired by Lord Brabazon and consisting of influential figures from the industry, was charged with determining the types of aircraft that Britain would need for post-war operations. With no clear indication of when the war was likely to end, this was certainly no easy task. Their recommendations led to a mixed bag of commercial failures and successes, ranging from the huge but unviable Bristol Brabazon to the very competitive Vickers Viscount and de Havilland Dove airliners. Yet, despite this commendable endeavour, at this time the nation's efforts were entirely geared to the forthcoming invasion of mainland Europe. Britain's aircraft production was now at its peak, mainly in support of the RAF's nightly pounding of German cities carried out alongside the equally relentless daylight raids conducted by the US Army Air Force.

When the war ended in Europe, it was intended that part of the RAF's bomber force would be redeployed as Tiger Force to the Far East to assist the American air attacks on Japan. Accordingly, work was put in hand to convert 600 Lancasters and 600 Lincoln bombers into tankers and receivers for air refuelling. In the event, the capture of islands that put Japan within unrefuelled range of the USAAF's B-29 bomber, coupled with its capitulation after the dropping of two atomic bombs, rendered British assistance unnecessary.

In the later stages of the war in Europe, the RAF received its first jet-propelled Meteor fighters, which though never engaging directly with their German counterpart, the Messerschmitt Me 262, nevertheless played an important part in combating the V1 flying bomb menace then threatening London and southern England. Although not yet employed on a large scale, jet power was clearly the propulsive force for the future and British engine makers were foremost in addressing the new challenge.

Advertising throughout the war was used to great effect as propaganda, aimed at boosting the country's morale. Companies were keen to see their products connected in some way to victorious events, their advertisements invariably having moved on from tranquil peacetime images to aggressive symbolism. It should be noted, however, that whilst the services and industry at large were able to remain constantly within the public eye, several other organisations that made a massive contribution to aviation throughout the war were unable, for security reasons, to advertise their skills. The most notable of these were the highly secret government testing and research establishments at Boscombe Down, Farnborough, Bedford and elsewhere, and the band of civilian pilots within the Air Transport Auxiliary who, it should be noted, ferried aircraft from the manufacturers to the RAF squadrons with appreciable loss of life.

SERVICE RECRUITING AND PROPAGANDA

This collection of advertising posters is typical of the general 'call to arms' that overtook the United Kingdom after the outbreak of the Second World War. As would be expected, the RAF had to make its appeal alongside similar recruiting campaigns waged by the Army and Royal Navy. There is, however, little doubt that the ability to 'strike back' in a seemingly glamorous and personal sense against the Nazi aggressor weighed heavily in the minds of those volunteering for aircrew duties.

1   RAF recruiting poster, *c.*1939.
2   RAF recruiting poster, *c.*1939.
3   RAF recruiting poster, *c.*1941.
4   RAF recruiting poster, *c.*1941.

Get into the air and *FIGHT!*

The Battle of Germany will be far fiercer than the Battle of Britain. It, too, must end in victory for the R.A.F. You with the fighting spirit, you too will want to be "in" — doing this grand job, full of adventure — getting the chance of a real crack at the enemy! Even if you are in a "reserved" job you can still volunteer for flying duties. And you who are being *de-reserved* and are thoroughly fit — even if you didn't express preference for R.A.F. flying duties when you registered for National Service with your age group — *you can volunteer now*, provided you are not yet posted to another Service. Men are wanted as Pilots (age under 31), Observers (age under 33). Pay, allowances and living conditions are good.

Volunteer for flying duties at the R.A.F. Section of your nearest Combined Recruiting Centre (address from any Employment Exchange), or post coupon for full details (unsealed envelope— 1d. stamp).

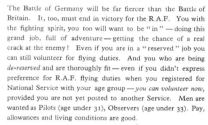

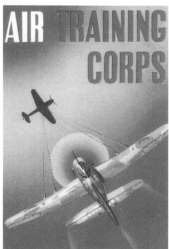

5 RAF recruiting poster, *c.*1942.
6 Ministry of Supply poster, 1942.
7 *Flight*, 22 January 1942.
8 RAF recruiting poster, *c.*1943.
9 ATC recruiting poster, *c.*1943.
10 RAF recruiting poster, *c.*1943.
11 RAF recruiting poster, *c.*1945.

THE AIRCRAFT CONSTRUCTORS

AIRSPEED (1934) LIMITED (ORIGINALLY AIRSPEED LIMITED)

In June 1940, the de Havilland Aircraft Company bought the Swan Hunter shareholding in Airspeed. This take-over, coupled with the effects of bombing raids on Portsmouth, led to the move to Hatfield of the company's design team, and the construction of a shadow factory at Christchurch. Throughout these upheavals, as the advertisements show, work continued on the production of some 1,500 Oxford trainer and communications aircraft and, later in the war, the Horsa glider. In 1944, with the company's name having again reverted to Airspeed Limited, project design studies were put in hand for a DC-3 replacement in line with the Brabazon Committee's Type 2 (later Type 2A) recommendations. This was later to become the Ambassador airliner.

1   *The Aeroplane,* 13 September 1940.
2   *Flight,* 12 December 1940.
3   *Flight,* 7 October 1943.
4   *Flight,* 21 September 1939.

SIR W G ARMSTRONG WHITWORTH AIRCRAFT LIMITED

Following a succession of civil airliners such as the Argosy, Atalanta and Ensign, the company renewed its entry into the military market with the A.W.23 transport, which proved to be the forerunner of the Whitley heavy bomber. The company advertisement shown here appears to depict Whitleys in a dive-bombing attack, a role for which they were most decidedly unsuited! Armstrong's other main wartime product, the Albemarle, did not fulfil its intended role as a reconnaissance bomber, being overtaken by the larger four-engined aircraft. However, 600 were built for glider towing and transportation of combat troops.

1

2

3

A.V. ROE AND COMPANY LIMITED

This selection of Avro advertisements portrays a distinctly aggressive tone – but not without justification, for within days of war breaking out in September 1939, an Anson 1 of 500 Squadron had bombed a German U-boat and a similar machine had, as depicted here, shot down a Dornier Do 18 flying-boat. A little later in the war, Ansons employed on coastal patrol accounted for several other enemy aircraft. The re-design of the ill-fated, twin-engined Manchester to become the world-beating Lancaster is, perhaps, too well known to need detailed recounting here. However, the great daylight raid by Lancasters on the Le Creusot arms factory on 17 October 1942 inspired the awesome strength of Bomber Command being vividly portrayed in the company's promotional material.

4

5

1   *Flight*, 12 December 1940.
2   *The Aeroplane*, 5 June 1942.
3   *Flight*, 11 March 1943.
4   *Flight*, 2 September 1943.
5   *Flight*, 30 September 1943.

BLACKBURN AIRCRAFT LIMITED

Shown here are the Botha, originally designed as a reconnaissance bomber, which was plagued by performance shortcomings and soon relegated to aircrew training duties, and the Skua fighter-dive bomber. Though charged with providing fighter protection of convoys and enjoying temporary fame in becoming the first British type to destroy an enemy aircraft on 25 September 1939, the Skua was more renowned for carrying out the classic dive-bombing attack which sank the German cruiser *Königsberg* in Bergen Harbour on 10 April 1940. The Roc, a dorsal-mounted, four-gun turret version of the Skua, was soon proved to be outmoded and unsuccessful as a fleet fighter, this role then being taken over by the Fairey Fulmar and the Grumman Martlet. Meanwhile, much effort was given to the sub-contracted production of Swordfish, Barracuda and Sunderland aircraft.

It was not until the later stages of the war that Blackburn re-emerged as a major design company in its own right, with the Firebrand to challenge its main competitor – Fairey!

1 *The Aeroplane,* 17 October 1941.
2 *Flight,* 7 October 1943.
3 *Flight,* 30 November 1944.

1

2

3

BOULTON PAUL AIRCRAFT LIMITED

The company's hopes of becoming a supplier of front-line fighter aircraft were dashed when it committed itself to producing the Defiant, a four-gun turret design that ranked alongside similarly configured and ill-fated machines, such as the Hawker Hotspur and Blackburn Roc.

With the Wolverhampton firm's wartime work later concentrated on the assembly of Halifax bombers and Fairey Barracudas, it was perhaps paradoxical that production of the company's successful range of gun turrets was transferred to Lucas company factories at Birmingham and Cwnbran in south Wales. The Defiant, however, when relieved of its day-fighter duties, did go on to become an adequate interim night-fighter and target-tug workhorse.

1 *Flight,* 8 February 1940.
2 *The Aeroplane,* 20 June 1941.

THE BRISTOL AEROPLANE COMPANY LIMITED

The Royal Air Force relied very heavily on the Bristol Company's aircraft in the earlier part of the war. Accordingly, its advertising centred on the Bombay bomber transport and the Blenheims, Beauforts and Beaufighters serving in Bomber, Coastal and Fighter Commands. As the nature of the bombing campaign changed in 1943 to place more emphasis on heavy four-engined aircraft, the company, having pursued similar designs, was asked to consider creating a vastly larger machine capable of carrying a massive bomb load of 80,000lb. This did not materialise, but the design experience gained in the exercise proved valuable in allowing Bristol to put forward schemes for a post-war transatlantic airliner. The company's proposals led directly to the manufacture of the Brabazon.

1   *The Aeroplane*, 5 June 1942.
2   *Flight*, 11 February 1943.

2

1

2

3

CUNLIFFE-OWEN AIRCRAFT LIMITED

Based at Southampton's airport, Cunliffe-Owen was, in the pre-war years, at the forefront of innovative aircraft design. The company's conviction that the 'flying wing' represented the way forward was certainly ahead of its time, for the basic concept has subsequently been shown to be sound and is now an inherent component in the design of today's stealth airframes. In the Second World War, however, official thinking would not allow any radical approach to interfere with the supply of more conventional designs. Accordingly, Cunliffe-Owen found itself the receiver and assembler of American-designed aircraft, a task it completed exceedingly well throughout the war-torn years.

1 *Flight*, 8 February 1940.
2 *The Aeroplane*, 13 September 1940.
3 *Aircraft of the Fighting Powers* vol. II (1941).
4 *Flight*, 22 January 1942.
5 *Aircraft of the Fighting Powers* vol. IV (1943).

4

5

DE HAVILLAND AIRCRAFT/ ENGINES/PROPELLERS LIMITED

A name to truly conjure with! However, despite its pre-war reputation, it appears that de Havilland did not invest in excessive wartime self-promotion. Nevertheless, the vital roles of the Tiger Moth trainer, the Mosquito and the de Havilland Engine and Propeller Companies cannot be overstated.

1   *Flight,* 28 January 1943.
2   *Flight,* 22 July 1943.
3   *Flight,* 29 July 1943.
4   *Aeronautics,* September 1944.

1

2

3

4

1

2

FAIREY AVIATION COMPANY LIMITED

Fairey's long association with naval aviation continued to be reflected in its wartime advertising. Of particular interest is the company's temporary departure from illustrations typically depicting a warship background, to those of sea-creatures having inspired the names given to its carrier-borne aircraft.

1 *The Aeroplane*, 13 September 1940.
2 *Flight*, 12 December 1940.
3 *The Aeroplane*, 6 June 1941.
4 *The Aeroplane*, 5 June 1942.

3

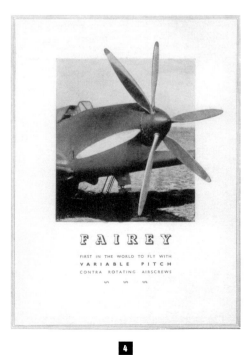

4

The "SWORDFISH"

The Ocean Gladiator. Widely distributed in the warm seas, and a mighty antagonist. There exist records of great sport with swordfish in the Straits of Messina about 100 B.C.

We have heard of their activities in this, and other areas, in more recent times.

FAIREY AIRCRAFT

The "FULMAR"

The Fulmar petrel is found around Britain's northern shores, and elsewhere. Of recent years its numbers have tended to increase.

Although gull-like in general appearance, its flight is distinctive.

FAIREY AIRCRAFT

THE "ALBACORE"

A species of tunny, and common in the Mediterranean. In spite of its size, it preys chiefly on the smaller fry, of which it eliminates large numbers.

FAIREY AIRCRAFT

THE "BARRACUDA"
THE WOLF OF THE SEAS

This ferocious torpedo-like fish, lurking in the obscure, delivers its attack with lightning rapidity. . . .

It attacks for the apparent delight of sheer destruction.

FAIREY AIRCRAFT

HONOURS IN ABUNDANCE
1939 – – 1945

'SEAFOX'
'BATTLE'
'SWORDFISH'
'ALBACORE'
'FULMAR'
'BARRACUDA'

THE FAIREY 'FIREFLY'

WON BY 9 TYPES OF
FAIREY AIRCRAFT

9

It happened at SUMATRA

In a recent series of brilliantly executed attacks, "Fairey Firefly" high performance reconnaissance fighters operating from British aircraft carriers wrecked vital oil refineries and radar stations occupied by the Japanese.

The Firefly is formidably armed with cannon guns, and can mount "the punch of a cruiser" in a heavy salvo of rocket projectiles.

The actions at Sumatra add new Battle Honours to the long list already achieved in Fairey naval aircraft.

The Fairey Aviation Company, only British company to design, develop and build large quantities aircraft exclusively for the Royal Navy throughout the war, is proud of the glorious feats achieved by the British Naval Air Arm.

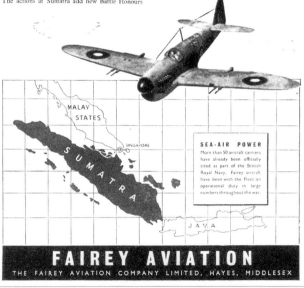

SEA-AIR POWER
More than 50 aircraft carriers have already been officially cited as part of the British Royal Navy. Fairey aircraft have been with the Fleet on operational duty in large numbers throughout the war.

FAIREY AVIATION
THE FAIREY AVIATION COMPANY LIMITED, HAYES, MIDDLESEX

10

It happened in JAPAN

All eyes were on Japan. And none more watchful than those of the Fairey Firefly aircrews who streaked from British carriers to pound and pulverise the Japanese war machine. Oil refineries, shipping, ammunition dumps, food stocks, radar stations, rolling stock — all on the list and all in the day's work for the Firefly long-range reconnaissance fighter, cited as the first British aircraft over Tokyo. With cannon guns, rocket projectiles, heavy bombs, impressive speed and exceptional manoeuvrability, the Firefly carries everything needed for attack.

The Fairey Aviation Company, only British Company to design, develop and build large quantities of aircraft exclusively for the Royal Navy throughout the war, is proud of its contribution to Victory — first in the West and now in the Far East.

FAIREY AVIATION
THE FAIREY AVIATION COMPANY LIMITED, HAYES, MIDDLESEX

11

5   *The Aeroplane*, 21 July 1944.
6   *The Aeroplane*, 22 December 1944.
7   *The Aeroplane*, 23 February 1945.
8   *The Aeroplane*, 9 March 1945.
9   *The Aeroplane*, 8 June 1945.
10 *The Aeroplane*, 24 August 1945.
11 *Flight*, 20 September 1945.

FOLLAND AIRCRAFT LIMITED

Though claiming, not unfairly, to be 'designers and manufacturers of aircraft', throughout the war Folland was almost entirely concerned with producing a vast range of sub-contracted components for sixteen different types of aircraft. The company also operated a Civilian Repair Organisation for the repair of damaged service aircraft, with sites located throughout the south and south-west of England. One of the company's more unusual tasks was to build and install floats for several Spitfire seaplane conversions. Twelve Folland F.43/37 specialist aircraft were also assembled for engine flight rest work.

1   *Flight*, 8 February 1940.

GENERAL AIRCRAFT LIMITED

This company, noted for its Monospar series of light general-purpose, pre-war machines, laid strong emphasis on its overseas sales when advertising. It is surprising, however, to see this aspect still being given optimistic prominence when Britain was fighting for survival in 1940! Wartime pre-occupation lay with the construction of Fairey Firefly naval fighters and a wide range of components and sub-assemblies for several other types in service. In addition to producing training machines equipped with a then unique tricycle undercarriage of its own design, the company became, alongside Airspeed, an important manufacturer of wartime gliders, such as the Hotspur and Hamilcar.

1   *The Aeroplane*, 13 September 1940.
2   *Flight*, 20 November 1942.
3   *The Aeroplane*, 26 January 1945.

1

2

GLOSTER AIRCRAFT COMPANY

The Gloster Company entered the war noted for having produced the Gladiator – the RAF's last biplane fighter. It ended the war having seen the introduction into service of its Meteor as Britain's first jet-propelled fighter. In between, sub-contracts were undertaken on other Hawker Siddeley Group designs, such as the Hawker Henley dive-bomber shown here.

The Gladiator's legendary role in Malta's valiant defence is well captured in this 1943 *Flight* advertisement, but the secrecy surrounding the development of the jet-engine meant that Gloster's pioneering efforts with the E.28/39, Britain's first jet-propelled aeroplane, were not made public until the end of the war.

3

4

1   *The Aeroplane*, 13 September 1940.
2   *Flight*, 12 December 1940.
3   Source uncertain, *c*.1940.
4   *Flight*, 29 August 1943.

THE HANDLEY PAGE COMPANY LIMITED

Following its move to Cricklewood in 1912, Handley Page was mainly identified throughout its long existence as a builder of medium and large-scale bomber aircraft. It would appear, however, that the company did not place a great reliance on advertising, no doubt believing that the excellence of its products would secure its own rewards! Nevertheless, following the Hampden's contribution to Britain's air war effort in the early period, the Halifax played a major role in the air offensive from March 1941 until the end of hostilities in Europe.

By 1945, with thoughts now directed to peacetime products, and looking beyond the passenger/freight conversion of the Halifax, Handley Page was beginning to advertise what would become the Hermes airliner.

1   *Flight,* 1 August 1940.
2   *Flight,* 22 May 1941.
3   *The Aeroplane,*
     17 October 1941.
4   *Flight,* 4 November 1943.
5   *The Aeroplane,* 20 April
     1945.

1

2

1 *Aeronautics*, January 1940.
2 *Flight*, 20 May 1943.

HAWKER AIRCRAFT LIMITED

This simplistic yet eye-catching advertisement is typical of a well-established company that perhaps feels its products almost sell themselves. It appeared in January 1940 just before the air war over France and Britain had really got underway. Just nine months later, Hawker would certainly have seen no requirement to press its claims through public advertising, the Hurricane having valiantly proved itself to be the RAF's mainstay fighter in both France and the Battle of Britain. The company went on to produce the excellent Typhoon and Tempest piston-engined successors to the Hurricane in the later stages of the war. However, its related advertising often concentrated on captioned photographs which, though excellent in themselves, were 'factual statements' as opposed to artistically inspired images.

1 *The Aeroplane*, 7 September 1939.
2 Source uncertain, *c*.1941.
3 *Country Life*, 30 April 1943.
4 *Country Life*, 18 February 1944.

MILES AIRCRAFT LIMITED

After finally separating from Phillips and Powis Aircraft Limited in 1943, Miles Aircraft Limited established its own fine reputation for advanced training aircraft. Note, however, the difference between the relative 'wordiness' of Miles advertisements and, say, those of Hawker Aircraft, which simply present a forceful product image. This might be taken to indicate the relative strengths and positions of the companies within the wartime airframe manufacturing 'league'.

1

2

3

4

PERCIVAL AIRCRAFT LIMITED

Although having produced a succession of first-rate light aircraft designs throughout the 1930s, Percival's own serious contribution to the war effort was production of the Proctor communications aircraft, some 1,300 being built at the company's Luton factory and at F. Hills and Sons in Manchester. In addition to this, Percival undertook the sub-contracted manufacture of many Oxford and Mosquito aircraft.

Though not given to flamboyant advertising during the austere war years, the company was, as illustrated here, looking toward the export market as peace drew near.

1

1   *The Aeroplane,* 20 April 1945.

SAUNDERS-ROE LIMITED

Though never short of foresight and innovative expertise related to marine aircraft, the company had to fall in line behind its arch-competitor, Shorts, throughout the war period. The Lerwick flying-boat, mainly operated by No.209 Squadron on operational patrols, proved to be an unpopular, controversial aircraft with a disappointing performance and was largely withdrawn from service in 1942. Despite these failings, the company continued to confidently advertise its products, but with peace fast approaching by 1945, it made a firm yet critically mistaken decision to dominate a self-promoted 'jumbo-scale' flying-boat market with its Princess flying-boat.

1   *Flight,* 8 February 1940.
2   Flight, 9 February 1945.

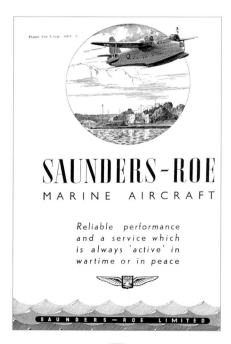

1

2

SHORT BROTHERS

As with the other heavyweight companies, Shorts seemed to have had little need to elaborate on the qualities of its products. However, the Stirling bomber, forever limited by the Air Ministry specification requirement for it to pass within a hangar door width of 100ft, inherited a serious operational height limitation. This exposed the aircraft to enemy ground fire, far more than its contemporary warriors the Lancaster and Halifax. Nevertheless, it was the RAF's first modern four-engined bomber and it generally acquitted itself well in various roles throughout the war. The Stirling's company stable mate, the Sunderland flying-boat, was the main coastal and convoy patrol aircraft employed by RAF Coastal Command, its virtues requiring little expansion in the company's advertising. In parallel with Saunders-Roe's approach, Shorts saw the Shetland flying boat as its immediate entry to a post-war civil air transport system highly dependent on water-borne aircraft.

1

2

SHORT BROTHERS

1   *The Aeroplane*, 13 September 1940.
2   *Flight*, 12 December 1940.
3   Short Brothers' Brochure, *c*.1941.

3

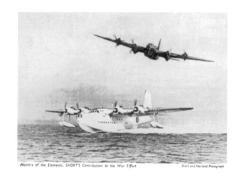

4 *Flight,* 28 August 1941.
5 *Flight,* 22 January 1942.
6 *Flight,* 6 April 1944.
7 *Flight,* 8 February 1945.
8 *Flight,* 17 May 1945.

VICKERS-ARMSTRONGS LIMITED

To most people during the war, 'Supermarine' was the name directly associated with the Spitfire, although Vickers-Armstrongs Limited had, since 1938, taken over both Supermarine (Vickers) Limited and its then parent firm, Vickers (Aviation) Limited. This complex corporate relationship explains why Spitfires feature so strongly in this advertisement, which appeared in *The Aeroplane* at the time the Battle of Britain was reaching its climax. The Wellington and Warwick were wartime aircraft far more closely identified with the Vickers manufacturing centre at Weybridge.

1   *Flight*, 1 August 1940.
2   *The Aeroplane*, 13 September 1940.

WESTLAND AIRCRAFT LIMITED

Of the three Westland designs manufactured during the war, the Lysander is the best known, having proved to be in a class of its own for army co-operation duties and the transporting of Special Operations Executive agents to and from occupied Europe. Less successful, however, was the company's Whirlwind fighter-bomber, which, though shown here in an aggressive attacking manoeuvre, equipped only two RAF squadrons before being withdrawn from service. Of similar high-aspect ratio wing configuration, the Welkin was designed to meet the threat of high-flying Luftwaffe bombers. When these failed to materialise, official interest waned and the type never entered squadron service. However, the prototypes were used to develop Westland's unique cabin pressurisation system, which led to the formation of what is now Honeywell Normalair Garrett Limited.

In addition to producing its own designs, Westland was a major sub-contracted supplier of Spitfires and Seafires throughout the war.

1   *Flight,* 12 December 1940.
2   *Aircraft of the Fighting Powers* vol. I (1940).
3   *Flight,* 24 December 1942.
4   *Aircraft of the Fighting Powers* vol. IV (1943).

1

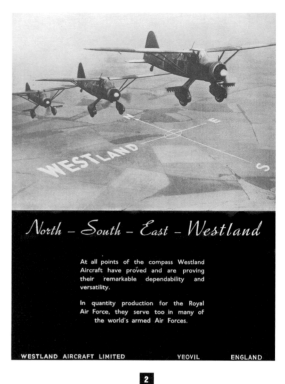

2

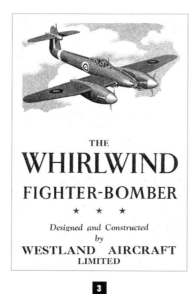

3

4

NAPIER ENGINES FOR HIGHER SPEED!

1

Bristol AERO ENGINES.

BRITAIN'S POWER IN THE SKIES.

2

THE ENGINE MAKERS

During the war, the supply of British aero-engines was centred on a small number of companies: Rolls-Royce, Bristol, Armstrong Siddeley, Napier and Blackburn.

As with its aeroplane advertising, Bristol produced strong images when publicising its engines. It should be noted, however, that the Bristol Aeroplane Company's Engine Department was re-formed as Bristol Aero Engines Limited in 1944. Also included in this 'power plant' selection is a typical advertisement for Rotol, a specialist airscrew company which combined the names of Rolls-Royce and Bristol. As an added comment, it appears strange (to the author at least) that the Blackburn Aircraft Company's name is absent in the promotion of its Cirrus engine!

1   *Flight*, 9 November 1939.
2   *Flight*, 3 March 1940.
3   *The Aeroplane*, 13 September 1940.
4   *The Aeroplane*, 17 October 1941.
5   *The Aeroplane*, 17 October 1941.

CIRRUS

150 H.P. CIRRUS "MAJOR"
90 H.P. CIRRUS "MINOR"

3

EFFICIENCY · ECONOMY · RELIABILITY · SIMPLICITY · DURABILITY

ARMSTRONG SIDDELEY

CHEETAH ENGINES

ARMSTRONG SIDDELEY MOTORS LTD. (BRANCH OF HAWKER SIDDELEY AIRCRAFT CO. LTD.)

4

"THE POWER BEHIND"

ROTOL

VARIABLE PITCH
AIRSCREWS

ROLLS-ROYCE   *Bristol*
ROTOL

Give generously to the R.A.F. Benevolent Fund.

5

6

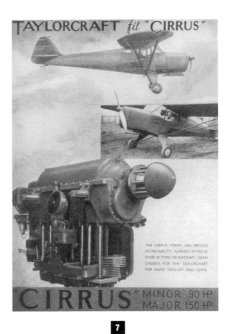

7

6   *The Aeroplane*, 27 February 1942.
7   *The Aeroplane*, 5 June 1942.
8   *The Aeroplane*, 21 August 1942.
9   *Flight*, 11 February 1943.

8

9

1

2

THE GENERAL EQUIPMENT PROVIDERS

Although limited here to but a small selection of equipment providers, a wide range of advertising styles is readily apparent. Several companies clearly relied on the tried and trusted patriotic appeal, while others maintained a conservative approach in emphasising the practical qualities of their products. Some companies were already looking beyond the end of the war with futuristic predictions, although at this stage very few advertisements were being reproduced in colour.

3

4

1   *The Aeroplane*, 17 September 1940.
2   *The Aeroplane*, 17 September 1940.
3   *Flight*, 17 July 1943.
4   *Flight*, 22 July 1943.

COTTON
BAGS

*For Aircraft Spare Parts
and Tube-End Covers*

WALTER H. FELTHAM & SON, LTD.
IMPERIAL WORKS, TOWER BRIDGE ROAD, LONDON, S.E.1

7

5

6

8

9

10

5 *Aeronautics*, July 1943.
6 *The Aeroplane*, 24 September 1943.
7 *Aircraft of the Fighting Powers* vol. IV (1943).
8 *The Aeroplane*, 7 January 1944.
9 *The Aeroplane*, 7 January 1944.
10 *The Aeroplane*, 18 May 1945.

1 *Flight,* 30 September 1943.
2 *Flight,* 31 May 1945.

THE PAINT AND FINISH SUPPLIERS

Selected especially for their evocative artistic appeal and, of course, the rare distinctive use of colour, are these advertisements for Titanine's aircraft finishes. 'Won't it look grand?' – It certainly did, but this was an essential effect for a company determined to provide a strong finish!

1

2

A WORLD OF DIFFERENCE, 1945–2008

The transition from war to peace in 1945 brought with it further serious challenges for Britain's aviation industry. Just as the end of the First World War had caused immediate large reductions in service manpower, so again the country's employment centres now had to meet a heavy demand for too few jobs. The services, however, faced a special problem, for although it was only fair that highly trained personnel with several long years of wartime service should be granted early demobilisation, the country still had strong military commitments in Europe and the Middle and Far East. In addition, the Soviet Communist bloc was already posing a threat to the western nations that would soon develop into the so-called 'Cold War'. Accordingly, between 1947 and 1963, National Service was introduced as a means of bolstering the strength of the armed forces. Meanwhile, the aircraft manufacturing companies, though no longer required to produce such large numbers of machines, still found it necessary to retain strong design teams for what would become a steady stream of new and advanced projects, both civil and military. Some of these were the direct result of the wartime Brabazon Committee's recommendations for five types of aircraft, ranging from a non-stop London–New York express airliner to a small feeder transport for internal services. To meet the first requirement, the Bristol Aeroplane Company constructed the massive Brabazon that was intended to provide sleeping berth accommodation for fifty passengers. However, political, financial and technical complications led to the abandonment of this impressive project after some 400 hours of prototype test flying. The Saunders-Roe Princess flying-boat was another highly ambitious large aircraft, which, though majestic to behold in flight, soon proved to be a commercial failure. Conceived in the latter stages of the war, though not as a result of the Brabazon Committee's findings, the Princess reflected the company's misplaced conviction that the large flying-boat had a significant future in civil air transportation. It was even envisaged that the turbo-propeller-engined Princess would later be overtaken by an all-jet-powered development that would be impressively titled the Saunders-Roe Duchess. None of this was to be, however, for whilst such waterborne airliner schemes were probably influenced by the pre-war 'by flying-boat to the Empire' style of thinking, the war had produced vast acres of concrete

runways that allowed direct inter-city connections without the need for extra internal travel from an arrival base inconveniently situated somewhere on the coast. However, smaller flying-boats, mainly derived from the wartime Short Sunderland, were still used by British Overseas Airways Corporation on the South African and Australasian routes until 1950, when the airline terminated all such operations.

Whilst conventional propeller and turbo-propeller driven aircraft clearly had ongoing roles to play, the late 1940s saw the turbo-jet engine take its place as the propulsive key to high-speed flight. Such engines powered the Gloster Meteor (1945 and 1946), Supermarine Swift (1953) and Hawker Hunter (1953) when each gained subsonic world airspeed records before Fairey test pilot Peter Twiss captured the supersonic prize in 1956, flying the company's F.D.2 at 1,132 mph. These achievements were gained either side of the political decision made in 1947 to cancel the potentially supersonic Miles M.52 piloted research aircraft and largely to confine the further exploration of transonic speeds to unmanned vehicles. Up until then, on a par with American research, the British, having passed its jet engine data to the US in the pressing interests of wartime co-operation, now found foreign competition moving ahead. Notwithstanding this, research into the high-subsonic regions still continued in this country with, for example, de Havilland building the swept-wing, tailless DH.108 Swallow, which was also intended to provide valuable basic aerodynamic data for the company's projected (and originally tailless) Comet airliner. As is well known, on 2 May 1952 this beautiful machine carried out the world's first pure-jet flight with fare-paying passengers between London and Johannesburg, only later to suffer a series of disastrous in-flight structural failures that involved severe loss of life and the grounding of the fleet. It was whilst de Havilland and the Royal Aircraft Establishment's scientific team at Farnborough were investigating the cause of the failures that America's Boeing Company introduced the 707 to the world's airlines. De Havilland, to its eternal credit, did produce excellent later variants of the Comet, but the head start in subsonic jet transport held by Britain at the start of the 1950s was never to be recovered. Despite these reversals the industry proved its resilience and determination to regain a leading position in civil transportation, with the preparation of designs for a supersonic airliner. As the decade progressed, Britain and France combined similar proposals in what became aviation's first major national collaborative project – Concorde. Continually plagued by political vacillations and concerns regarding its environmental suitability, the aircraft, which left its American rivals firmly grounded, and though brilliantly fulfilling all the specification technical requirements, was limited to flagship service with British Airways and Air France from 1976 until its final farewell in 2003. Nevertheless, the ability of the European partners to successfully manage such a highly complex project provided the vital confidence to undertake subsequent joint national military aircraft ventures such as the Sepecat Jaguar, Panavia Tornado, Eurofighter and the Airbus series of airliners. Among the British industry's mixed bag of successes and failures, the Vickers Viscount stands out as a milestone in civil air transport. It was the first turbo-propeller-engined aeroplane to operate a revenue passenger service, and with 445 examples eventually being sold, it fully underlined the Brabazon Committee's foresight. Not so fortunate was the Fairey Aviation Company's revolutionary Rotodyne. This tip-jet-assisted rotary-wing design, though not a Brabazon Committee recommendation, held great promise, with British European Airways keen to achieve central inter-city travel well ahead of its rivals, but the concept proved to be ahead of its time.

On the military side, English Electric produced the Canberra bomber which, in addition to serving with many of the world's air forces, remained in operational use with the RAF from 1951 until 2006. Throughout the 1950s and 1960s, British companies produced outstanding and innovative aircraft and weaponry that were truly world class. One need look no further than the V-bomber series of Valiant, Vulcan and Victor to find long-range nuclear striking power and subsequent tanker capability at its most impressive, whilst the Javelin and Lightning represented a breakthrough in British all-weather and rapid-climb interceptor design. However, in 1957, when the Conservative Government made its pronouncement that henceforth the RAF would not receive any more manned fighters, it dealt a severe blow not only to service morale, but to the industry itself. A total reliance on ground-to-air missiles, such as the Bloodhound and Thunderbird, for the nation's defence later proved to be misplaced, and resulted in a critically uncertain ten-year phase that included the cancellation of the supersonic Harrier, before the next generation of manned fighters eventually entered service. It was, however, during the post-war period that three major technical innovations were introduced. The first was the probe-and-drogue method of air refuelling devised by Sir Alan Cobham's team at Flight Refuelling Limited in 1949. The increases it provided in range and payload, and in some cases the need for fewer aircraft to undertake a mission, vastly improved service capabilities. Today's military air movements and missions continue to be highly dependent on the ability to refuel in flight.

Many an aircrew member would rate the second British invention, the Martin-Baker ejection seat, as the most important, for over the past fifty years it has saved well over 7,000 lives – and still counting!

The third technical advance to warrant special mention is the VTOL/STOL (vertical/short take-off and landing) concept, jointly developed by Sir Sydney Camm's Hawker Siddeley design team and that of Sir Stanley Hooker at Rolls-Royce. Initially demonstrated on the Hawker P.1127 in July 1961, the swivelling exhaust nozzles were later shown to give crucial added manoeuvrability to the Royal Navy's Sea Harriers when in combat during the Falklands campaign.

In addition to radar and the jet engine, each of these inventions is, in its own distinctive way, a prime example of British design ingenuity.

The post-war decades have seen the gradual contraction of the aircraft manufacturing industry through a series of take-overs and amalgamations. This is not, however, a situation unique to Britain, as changing times, political environments, service requirements and technological advances have imposed themselves on virtually every large company within the global aerospace community.

In this country the first serious spasm of corporate change came in the late 1950s and mid-1960s when most of the major airframe firms were absorbed into either Hawker Siddeley Aviation Limited or the British Aircraft Corporation, and the individual engine producers, Bristol, Armstrong Siddeley, Blackburn and de Havilland, merged into Rolls-Royce. The mid-1970s then saw both aircraft manufacturing groups come together to form the all-embracing British Aerospace plc, which, in 1999, then became BAe Systems. Westland has retained its relative independence for longer than most, but is now teamed with Agusta within the Italian Finmeccanica group. Shorts, the company with the longest association with British aviation, became government owned in 1943, but following its sale in 1989 is now the European group of its Canadian parent, Bombardier Aerospace Inc.

These have been just some of the 'ups and downs' of the aviation industry's rollercoaster ride in the post-war years, but significant changes have also taken place in the style of advertising used by aerospace companies. The specially commissioned paintings that had, for some thirty years, adorned the covers of *Flight* and *Aeroplane* and which appealed to the public and industry alike, were gone by the start of the 1970s. This is hardly surprising, for the individual firms that they represented had, by then, disappeared themselves.

Today, aerospace company advertising tends to be sharply directed via web-sites towards the industry's own professional sectors. Only at the major trade exhibitions and air shows held at Farnborough, Fairford, Paris, Dubai and around the world is a more general artistic appeal in evidence – which, one might wryly observe, is pretty much where this journey started out!

THE AIRCRAFT CONSTRUCTORS

AIRSPEED (1934) LIMITED

Airspeed (1934) Limited became Airspeed Limited on 25 January 1944. Despite the company name change, Airspeed still remained a wholly owned subsidiary within the de Havilland organisation. With its design team now established at Christchurch, company efforts were mainly directed to the AS.57, a high-speed trans–continental airliner aimed at meeting Brabazon Committee requirements. Clearly, great hopes were entertained for what was to become the Ambassador, as shown in the company's strong advertising campaign. British European Airways operated a fleet of twenty Ambassadors of the Elizabethan class until the type, facing severe economic competition from the turboprop Vickers Viscount, was withdrawn from service in 1958. On the other hand, the Airspeed Consul, a civil version of the Oxford trainer, proved to be a financially successful civil transport venture.

The company became the Airspeed Division of de Havilland in 1951, and soon after was simply known as The de Havilland Company, Christchurch, by which time work was concentrated on the DH 115 Vampire trainer, the DH 112 Venom and, later, the redesign of the DH 110, which in service became the Sea Vixen.

1   *The Aeroplane,* 10 March 1946.
2   *The Aeroplane,* 2 April 1948.
3   *The Aeroplane,* 14 May 1948.
4   *Flight,* 19 October 1951.

1

2

3

4

1

2

AUSTER AIRCRAFT LIMITED/BEAGLE AIRCRAFT LIMITED

This company was, perhaps, only rivalled by Phillips and Powis/Miles Aircraft in the complexity of its evolution. A descendant of the pre-war Taylorcraft Company, Auster Aircraft went on, after production of its military observation model throughout the war, to produce a wide range of variants for the civil flying club market, including Arrow, Autocrat and Aiglet. The company continued to manufacture the Air Observation Post MK9 model for Army co-operation duties until commercial pressures led, in 1969, to its merging with Miles Aircraft to become British Executive and General Aviation Limited – better known as 'Beagle'. Both companies' advertising style was crisp, simply defined and of the 'no-nonsense' school.

1 *The Aeroplane*, 10 September 1954.
2 *Flying Review International*, February 1969.

1

2

3

SIR W.G. ARMSTRONG WHITWORTH AIRCRAFT LIMITED

Though initially falling back on some retrospective advertising for the wartime Albemarle, Armstrong Whitworth's forward-looking policy lay with flying-wing designs.

Whilst British progress with the 'flying-wing' concept rested with the company 9and Cunliffe-Owen), work was also undertaken on the Apollo airliner and the four-engined, twin-boom A.W.660 Argosy military transport.

Armstrong Whitworth was a major sub-contractor for Sea Hawk, Hunter and Javelin fighters throughout the 1950s. The company was also engaged in ground-to-air missile design and production during its tenure as part of the Hawker Siddeley Group.

1 *Flight*, 30 January 1947.
2 *The Aeroplane*, 21 May 1948.
3 *Flight*, 29 May 1947.

4

5

6

4   *The Aeroplane,* 9 June 1950.
5   *Flight,* 9 December 1960.
6   Source uncertain, *c.*1962.

A.V. ROE AND COMPANY LIMITED

Thanks mainly to the Lancaster, Avro emerged from the war with an impeccable reputation. The company experienced a major setback, however, when its talented chief designer, Roy Chadwick, lost his life in the crash of the prototype Tudor 2 airliner on 23 August 1947. Despite flamboyant advertising, subsequent losses of the Tudor, when operated by British South American Airways, did little to encourage airline and public confidence, although the type did acquit itself well during the 1948-9 Berlin Airlift.

Rising above these early post-war problems, Avro re-established its former high ranking with, firstly, the Lincoln and, in the 1950s, the mighty Vulcan bomber. Alongside these bomber projects, work commenced on the latest marks of Anson, the Athena trainer, the Shackleton maritime reconnaissance aircraft and the Ashton research machines.

The Avro 748, which first appeared in 1958, later became the Hawker Siddeley H.S.748 turboprop airliner, proving very successful in the civil and (as the Andover) in the military medium transport roles.

1   *The Aeroplane,* 4 January 1946.
2   *The Aeroplane,* 8 February 1946.
3   *The Aeroplane,* 10 May 1946.
4   Source unknown, *c.*1947.

THE TUDOR SPIRIT LIVES AGAIN

THE AVRO TUDOR II

5

For *luxurious long-range travel*

THE AVRO TUDOR II

4 ROLLS-ROYCE MERLIN ENGINES

A.V. ROE & CO. LIMITED MANCHESTER (BRANCH OF HAWKER SIDDELEY AIRCRAFT CO. LIMITED)

6

5 *Flight*, 9 January 1947.
6 *Flight*, 5 June 1947.
7 Source uncertain, *c.*1948.
8 *The Aeroplane*, 16 April 1948.
9 *The Aeroplane*, 30 April 1948.

AIRCREW TRAINING....

The practical aspect of aircrew training is of major importance to any air force or airline. New Avro Anson trainers, now in service with the Royal Air Force, are proving the value of an adequate "flying classroom." This, on the score of economy alone, is worth careful study. Subject to variation from the standard installation, we can offer very good delivery terms for new aircraft.

AVRO ANSON 20

A V ROE & COMPANY LIMITED *(Branch of the Hawker Siddeley Group)*

7

THE *AVRO* **ATHENA** *ADVANCED TRAINER*

ROBUST CONSTRUCTION

EXCEPTIONAL ACCESSIBILITY } MORE FLYING HOURS

COMPONENT INTERCHANGEABILITY

8

LIAISON
BY LINCOLN

Flights of friendship and liaison rate high in the Air Council's programme of co-operation with the Commonwealth Air Forces, and Avro aircraft have been chosen for many of these missions. Recently the Empire Radio School's ' Mercury II ', a standard Lincoln bomber with additional radio equipment, has visited Australia, New Zealand and the Middle and Far East. The Empire Air Armament School and the Central Bomber Establishment have also sent out parties to South Africa and Southern Rhodesia in the Lincolns ' Thor II ' and ' Crusader ', while the flight of the Empire Air Navigation School's Lincoln ' Aries II ' to Australia and New Zealand last October was typical of the many goodwill missions to other countries on which Lincolns have been flown. Constantly on the move along the air routes of the Commonwealth, these Avro Lincoln have proved their outstanding reliability and their ability to operate, as they were designed to do, under the most varying conditions of temperature and weather in all parts of the world.

A. V. ROE & CO LTD MANCHESTER

BRANCH OF HAWKER SIDDELEY AIRCRAFT CO LTD

9

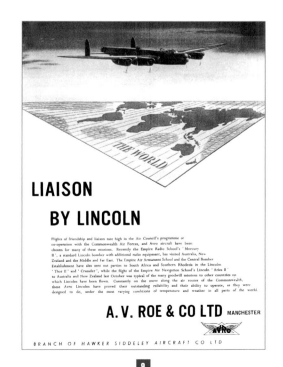

10

11

12

13

14

10   *The Aeroplane*, 18 June 1948.
11   *The Aeroplane*, 8 October 1948.
12   *The Aeroplane*, 22 April 1949.
13   *Flight*, 20 June 1958.
14   Source uncertain, *c.*1960.

BOULTON PAUL AIRCRAFT LIMITED

This company produced three aircraft designs of note in the post-war period. The Balliol advanced trainer was the only one to enter production, but its service life was effectively over by 1957, the piston-engined varient being overtaken by the need for jet trainers. The Boulton Paul PIII/IIIA and P.120 were research vehicles designed to investigate the control and stability of high-speed delta-wing configurations. These were, however, the final original designs produced by the company before it was merged into the Dowty Group of companies in 1961.

1   *The Aeroplane, c.*1949.

1

BLACKBURN AIRCRAFT LIMITED, GENERAL AIRCRAFT LIMITED, BLACKBURN AND GENERAL AIRCRAFT LIMITED

Much weight was given by Blackburn to advertising its Firebrand naval strike aircraft. This machine had its origins in a pre-war Air Ministry specification calling for a two-seat replacement for the Gladiator, Skua and Fulmar. The long, drawn-out procedure involved in the changes to operational role, power plant and structure meant, however, that the latest marks only entered service with the Royal Navy in mid-1945. By 1952, the type was replaced by the Westland Wyvern. High hopes were placed on a potential successor to the Firebrand, which, designed to Ministry Specification S.28/43, was unofficially named Firecrest. This, too, failed to secure naval interest, as did the Y.A.5/Y.B.1 anti-submarine aircraft, when the Fairey Gannet was selected as the preferred machine for such duties. At this time, Blackburn's role as a supplier of first-class naval aircraft was clearly threatened, but its N.A.39 Buccaneer high-speed, low-level bomber was to become the Royal Navy's mainstay airborne strike weapon throughout the 1960s and 1970s. This was before the RAF, already equipped with its own Buccaneers, was called upon to absorb a large number of the ex-naval squadron machines.

On 1 January 1949, General Aircraft Limited merged with Blackburn Aircraft Limited to form Blackburn and General Aircraft Limited. In so doing, work on what was originally General's Universal Freighter was gradually transferred from Feltham in Middlesex to Brough in East Yorkshire. Following the type's development as a military transport for the Royal Air Force, the name Beverley was adopted, following the usual practice of naming such machines after British towns and cities. The type was eventually retired from RAF squadron service in 1967, transport duties then being handed over to the Lockheed C-130 Hercules.

1   *Flight,* 13 December 1945.

2

3

2 *The Aeroplane*, 1 February 1946.
3 *Flight*, 13 February 1947.
4 *The Aeroplane*, 17 December 1948.
5 Blackburn and General Aircraft brochure, *c.*1949.
6 British Export catalogue, 1949.

4

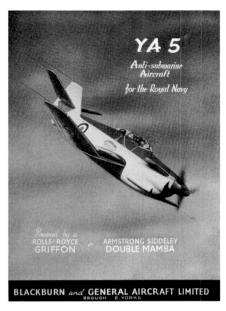

5

6

7

BLACKBURN YB1 AND GAL 60 AIRCRAFT
for Anti-submarine Duties & Military Transport

8

The *Blackburn Beverley*
*Transport Aircraft now in production
for the Royal Air Force*

Blackburn and General Aircraft Limited, Brough, E. Yorks

9

7 Blackburn and General Aircraft brochure, *c*.1950.
8 *The Aeroplane*, 24 November 1950.
9 Blackburn and General Aircraft brochure, *c*.1956.
10 Source uncertain, *c*.1956.

Mobility . . .
the keynote of modern strategy . . .
is provided by

the *Beverley*

in production for the
Royal Air Force

Blackburn and General Aircraft Limited, Brough, E. Yorks

10

11   *The Aeroplane*, 7 September 1956.
12   *The Aeroplane*, 14 December 1956.

On the approach — the NA.39 Strike Aircraft
BLACKBURN & GENERAL AIRCRAFT LIMITED

13

13 *Flight,* 14 February 1958.
14 *Flight,* 12 September 1958.

14

THE CONGLOMERATES: BRITISH AIRCRAFT CORPORATION, BRITISH AEROSPACE, BAE SYSTEMS, HAWKER SIDDELEY GROUP, HAWKER SIDDELEY AVIATION

After early moves began in 1928, the Hawker Siddeley Group was formally constituted in 1935, bringing together A.V. Roe, Hawker, Gloster, Armstrong Whitworth and Air Service Training. This coincided with the beginning of the massive shadow factory and aircraft production expansion schemes set up to meet the growing possibility of war. Each individual company continued to advertise its products under its own name, with minimal public reference to the parent organisation until after the war, when, in 1963, more companies were merged into what had become Hawker Siddeley Aviation.

Just prior to this, in 1960, most of the remaining major companies within the industry were swept up into a rival conglomerate, the British Aircraft Corporation. In 1977, both organisations were, in turn, brought together to form British Aerospace (BAe), before a final condensation of this and the defence interests of GEC (Marconi Electronic Systems) resulted in the creation of BAe Systems in 1999. Running alongside this rationalisation of the fixed-wing industry was the gradual merging of the rotorcraft companies to become, firstly, Westland Helicopters Limited, then GKN Westland Helicopters Limited and what is now Agusta Westland.

These amalgamations, whilst no doubt necessary to provide strong British competition in the world's aviation markets, nevertheless saw a marked change in the corporate advertising style. Paintings and impressions largely now gave way to images which, though often brilliant examples of the photographers' art, had a more sharp-edged but, in the author's opinion, less esoteric appeal.

1   *The Aeroplane*, 5 November 1946.
2   *Flight*, 21 November 1946.
3   *The Aeroplane*, 5 September 1947.

4

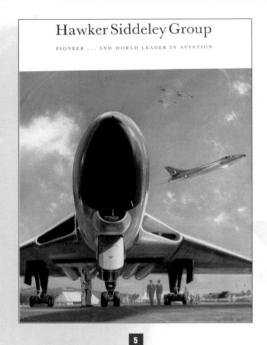

5

6

7

8

4 Hawker Siddeley Group in-house magazine, 1953.
5 *The Aeroplane*, 31 August 1956.
6 RAF Flying Review, *c.*1960.
7 Source uncertain, *c.*1962.
8 *Flight*, 21 June 1962..

9

10

11

12

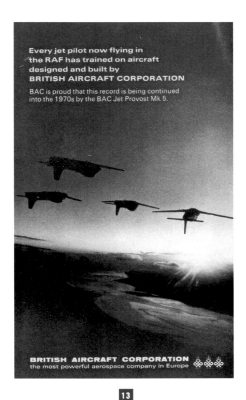

13

14

15

9   *Flight*, 1 January 1960.
10   *Flight*, 18 June 1970.
11   Source uncertain, *c.*1966.
12   *Flight*, 28 March 1968.
13   RAF Display Programme, Colerne, 17 June 1972.
14   International Air Tattoo programme, 1995.
15   British Aircraft Corporation sales brochure, late 1960s.

THE BRISTOL AEROPLANE COMPANY LIMITED/BRISTOL AIRCRAFT LIMITED

As the company's advertisement claimed, Bristol's aim in the immediate post-war years was to commence a new chapter in the history of aviation, with the massive Brabazon airliner as its chosen instrument.

Unfortunately, the airline's pre-war policy of carrying an elite few in great comfort was soon shown to be outdated, with everyday crossings of the Atlantic by the latest range of American transport aircraft such as the Constellation, Stratocruiser and the Douglas D.C.7, each carrying a significantly large number of passengers in reasonable comfort. For a brief period, however, as the 1940s became the 1950s, the mighty Brabazon, along with its equally large flying-boat contemporary, the Saunders Roe Princess, held centre stage, both appearing to point the way forward for British civil transportation. The advertising supporting both these leviathan projects was intense and impressive and, in Bristol's case, well exceeded that undertaken to promote the far more deserving 'maid of all work' Wayfarer short-haul airliner.

After absorbing the disappointment of the Brabazon, and prior to becoming part of the British Aircraft Corporation in 1960, the company produced the elegant Britannia airliner, the Sycamore and Belvedere military helicopters and the Type 188 high-speed research aircraft – the last true Bristol type to fly.

1   *The Aeroplane*, 22 May 1946.
2   *Flight*, 2 March 1950.
3   *The Aeroplane*, 19 September 1952.
4   *Flight*, 13 January 1956.

1

2

3

4

1 *Flight,* 11 September 1947.

THE CIERVA AUTOGIRO COMPANY LIMITED

Following the death of the Spanish inventor of the autogiro, Juan de la Cierva, in a fixed-wing aircraft crash at Croydon in 1938, interest in the freely rotating rotor autogiro soon declined, but his company continued to become involved with early helicopter projects in Britain. The Cierva Company's most ambitious project was the triple-rotor Air Horse, which first flew at Eastleigh in December 1948. Tragically, the sole example of this unique machine crashed on 13 June 1950, taking the lives of all its crew. As the advertising shows, the concept, with large-scale helicopter projects then in their infancy, promised a novel approach to bulk transportation.

CUNLIFFE-OWEN AIRCRAFT LIMITED

Despite its excellent wartime record as an assembler of American aircraft, Cunliffe-Owen failed to make progress in the post-war aviation market. Having discarded its forward-thinking 'lifting fuselage' policy, the company fell back on a more conventional approach to passenger-carrying with its Concordia feeder-liner. This project, however, proved to be a non-starter, along with those of other companies such as Armstrong Whitworth (Apollo) and, on a far larger scale, Bristol (Brabazon) and Saunders-Roe (Princess). Nonetheless, the company's colourful advertising represented an optimistic approach that was unfulfilled, mainly due to competition from the large stocks of war surplus DC.3 Dakotas.

1 *The Aeroplane,* 15 November 1946.

THE DE HAVILLAND AIRCRAFT COMPANY LIMITED

The arrival of peace in 1945 found the de Havilland organisation fully extended on a wide range of projects. Design and manufacture of the Hornet and Sea Hornet fighters ran alongside work on the excellent Dove and Heron transport variants and the Chipmunk trainer.

The company's Vampire twin-boom jet interceptor entered production in mid-1945 and became the first fighter of any nation to possess a top speed in excess of 500mph. The DH 108 Swallow was designed for high-speed research, but the price paid was high, the test programme resulting in the loss of all three prototypes and the death of each pilot.

The Comet airliner was initially hailed as the machine that would break America's stranglehold on passenger-carrying aircraft. In providing the world's first revenue-generating jet service, the prophecy appeared to be fulfilled but a tragic succession of crashes due to metal fatigue brought delays to the delivery programme that allowed the Boeing 707 to capture the world's airlines' interest – and orders! The later variants of Comet did go on to provide excellent service in both military and civil roles, but never to the extent that was at first foreseen. De Havilland's jet fighter line continued with the Venom, Sea Venom and Sea Vixen all entering service with either the RAF or Royal Navy. On the civil side, the Trident airliner was developed principally in accordance with requirements set out by British European Airways which, unfortunately, limited its appeal to other potential users.

Export sales of de Havilland aircraft, engines and propellers which, already excellent before the war, were similarly impressive in the post-war period and no doubt influenced in no small measure by the company's high-quality advertising, typified in the small selection shown here.

The de Havilland Vampire, a standard Royal Air Force combat aircraft which, with comprehensive military load, armament and full operational endurance, handsomely exceeds 500 m.p.h. in sustained level flight

1

2

3

4

1   *The Aeroplane,*
      9 November 1945.
2   *The Aeroplane,*
      6 February 1947.
3   *The Aeroplane,*
      7 February 1947.
4   *Flight, c.*1947.

DE HAVILLAND

REVERSIBLE PROPELLERS

FOR EASE OF MANŒUVRE

5

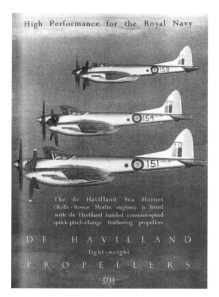

6

7

5   *The Aeroplane*, 11 July 1947.
6   *The Aeroplane*, 7 May 1948.
7   *The Aeroplane*, 7 May 1948.

A Dove on airline service between the islands of the Azores, one of thirty countries where this versatile, economical, proven feeder-liner is in daily operation

DE HAVILLAND DOVE

8

The finest introduction to sound airmanship

The de Havilland CHIPMUNK basic trainer

9

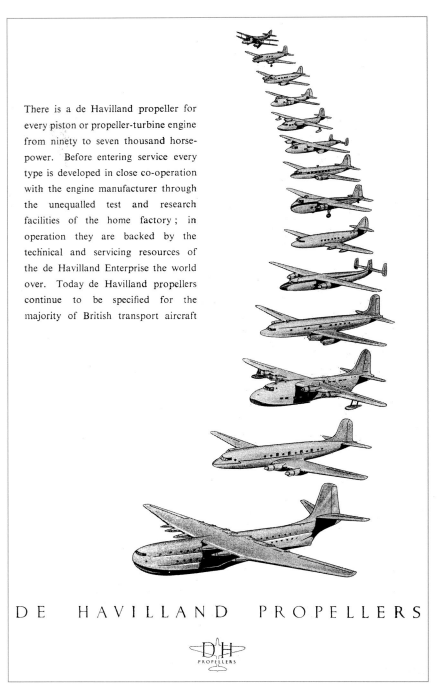

There is a de Havilland propeller for every piston or propeller-turbine engine from ninety to seven thousand horse-power. Before entering service every type is developed in close co-operation with the engine manufacturer through the unequalled test and research facilities of the home factory; in operation they are backed by the technical and servicing resources of the de Havilland Enterprise the world over. Today de Havilland propellers continue to be specified for the majority of British transport aircraft

DE HAVILLAND PROPELLERS

10

VAMPIRE NIGHT FIGHTER
setting a new world standard for defence by night

11

8   *The Aeroplane*, 8 October 1948.
9   *The Aeroplane*, 22 April 1949.
10   *The Aeroplane*, 14 April 1950.
11   Source uncertain, *c.*1951.
12   *Flight*, 9 January 1953.

SEA VENOM
(de Havilland Ghost jet engine)
In production for the Royal Navy

DE HAVILLAND

12

14

13

13 *The Aeroplane*, 15 October 1954.
14 De Havilland brochure, *c.*1960.

THE ENGLISH ELECTRIC COMPANY LIMITED/ENGLISH ELECTRIC AVIATION LIMITED

Following the relatively recent retirement of the last P.R.9 Canberras from RAF service, any sightings of this type will now wistfully be limited to the two machines presently owned by Air Atlantique putting in guest appearances at air shows. The Canberra proved to be a most remarkable aircraft, not only in being the English Electric Company's re-entry project into basic aircraft design, but also in becoming the first British jet bomber. Many variants ensued, contributing to well over fifty years of unbroken service with RAF squadrons and record overseas sales. The aircraft's clean lines were always beautifully portrayed in the company's advertising, and complemented the illustrations depicting the raw supersonic power of the Mach 2 Lightning and the functional simplicity of the firm's missile products.

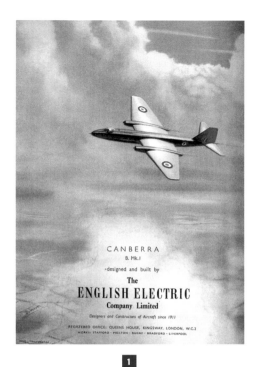

1   *The Aeroplane*, 9 June 1950.
2   *The Aeroplane*, 29 March 1957.
3   *The Aeroplane*, 29 March 1957.
4   *Flight*, 29 August 1958.

THE FAIREY AVIATION COMPANY LIMITED

The sheer inventiveness of British aviation companies over the first half-century of powered flight was well exemplified by Fairey Aviation. In covering the twenty years or so since the end of the Second World War, its products included the Firefly naval fighter, the Gyrodyne, Jet Gyrodyne and Ultra-Light helicopters, the Primer trainer, Gannet anti-submarine aircraft, the Delta One and Two research machines and the revolutionary Rotodyne vertical take-off airliner. Other activities included guided missile research and powered flying control development. It would indeed be difficult to record all of the company's achievements in this short space, but pride of place most certainly goes to the F.D.2 in securing the World Absolute Speed Record of 1,132mph in March 1956. Political decisions, however, prevented the development of this aircraft into a supersonic fighter – a role subsequently filled by the Dassault Mirage which proved such an export winner for the rival French company.

In 1959, the Fairey Company Limited was formed as a holding company for various subsidiaries, but the failure of orders for its advanced projects and the run down of Gannet production led to the takeover in 1969 by Westland Helicopters Limited.

Throughout its time as a front-line company, Fairey's advertising never failed to be varied, colourful and full of interest.

1   *The Aeroplane*, 8 February 1946.
2   *Flight*, 22 July 1948.
3   Source uncertain, c.1948.
4   *Flight*, 15 May 1955.

1

2

3

4

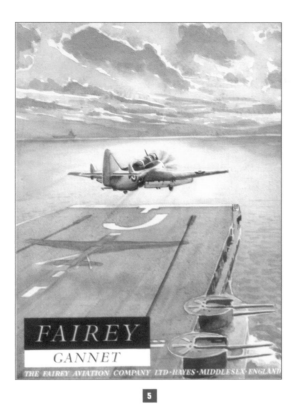

5

6

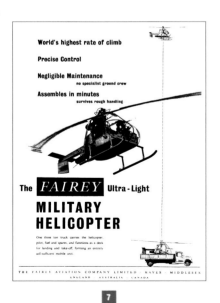

7

8

9

5   *The Aeroplane,*
     18 December 1953.
6   *Flight, c.*1955.
7   *The Aeroplane,*
     9 November 1956.
8   World's Press News,
     13 March 1957.
9   *The Aeroplane,*
     27 September 1957.

FOLLAND AIRCRAFT LIMITED

Though generally regarded as one of the smaller aviation companies, Folland, having engaged in sub-contract work throughout the war, grew in strength and capability in the post-war years. It produced, in 1954, the prototype Midge lightweight jet fighter. The production variant, the Gnat, followed a year later, the type proving very successful in service both at home and overseas. Though perhaps not setting great artistic standards, this small miscellany of advertisements reflects a compact, competent company that worked well, within its limited design and production capabilities.

DESIGNERS AND CONSTRUCTORS OF AIRCRAFT FOR ALL PURPOSES
CONTRACTORS TO THE AIR MINISTRY

HAMBLE
SOUTHAMPTON
HAMPSHIRE ENGLAND

1

Folland – pioneer in aircraft design for 35 years

HAMBLE   SOUTHAMPTON   HAMPSHIRE

2

"A great moment — and a great aeroplane for the occasion"

FOLLAND Gnat Trainer
Bristol Siddeley Orpheus
Ordered in quantity by the Royal Air Force

HAWKER SIDDELEY AVIATION *32 Duke Street, London, S.W.1.*

3

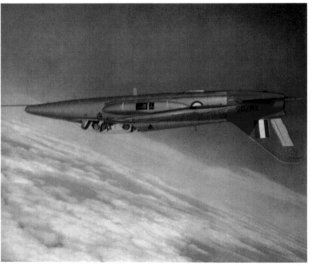

Folland Gnat – *the new advanced trainer for the Royal Air Force*

HAWKER SIDDELEY AVIATION 32 Duke St., St. James's, London S.W.1.

4

1 *Aircraft of the Fighting Powers* vol. VI, (1945)

2 *The Aeroplane,* 5 September 1947.

3 *Flight,* 9 December 1960.

4 *Flight,* September 1961.

THE GLOSTER AIRCRAFT COMPANY LIMITED

Gloster, Britain's pioneering jet aircraft manufacturer, soon gained notable post-war success when its Meteor IV gained the World Air Speed record in both 1945 (606mph) and 1946 (616mph). As more records were achieved, the company, naturally keen to capitalise on the type's jet capabilities, emphasised the speed aspect in its assertive advertising. As a first generation jet-fighter, the Meteor was an undoubted success not only with the RAF, but also serving with several major air forces overseas.

Overtaking the Meteor in the mid-1950s, the Gloster Javelin was a far more complicated heavyweight all-weather fighter. Along with the Lightning, it became the 'joint first' of the RAF's fighters to be capable of receiving fuel in the air for long-range deployment. Unsurprisingly, the aircraft's all-weather capabilities are strongly expressed in the advertising illustrations.

1 *The Aeroplane*, 29 March 1945.
2 *The Aeroplane*, 15 November 1946.
3 *The Aeroplane*, 3 January 1947.
4 *Flight*, 10 April 1947.

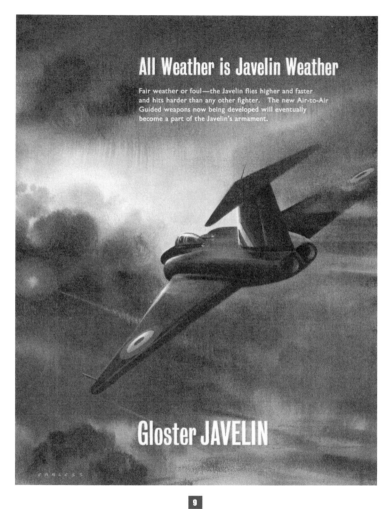

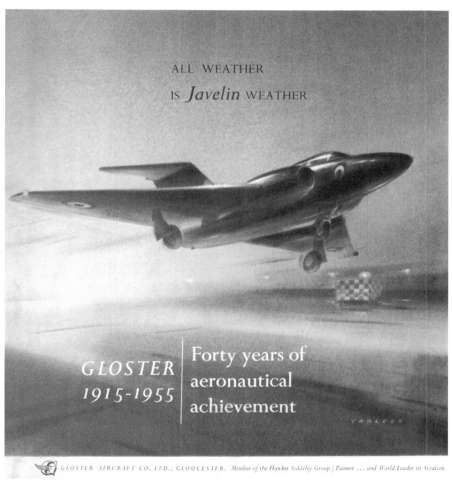

9   *Aeronautics*, November 1953.
10 *The Aeroplane*, 27 May 1955.

8   *The Aeroplane*, 24 November 1950.
9   *Aeronautics*, November 1953.
10 *The Aeroplane*, 27 May 1955.

HANDLEY PAGE LIMITED

The Handley Page Company, reflecting the stolid nature of its founder, Sir Frederick, remained until its demise a fiercely independent entity. Its post-war commercial transports were conventional, workman-like designs such as the Hastings and its civil counterpart, the Hermes, which served for some fourteen years in commercial service.

The company also took over the assets of Miles Aircraft when it faced liquidation in 1947, in a rescue act for the Marathon feeder-liner. This move resulted in the reconstitution of Handley Page Transport, dormant since 1924, as Handley Page (Reading) Limited.

Handley Page is, however, more famously associated with its own Herald and Jetstream civil aircraft and the unique crescent-winged Victor bomber, which was to serve for thirty years as the RAF's mainstay air tanker.

Although most of Britain's major airframe companies had, by the early 1960s, become part of the British Aircraft Corporation or Hawker Siddeley Aviation, Handley Page managed to retain its independence until, in 1970, it was finally absorbed into British Aerospace.

Not generally given to frivolity, as earlier stated, Handley Page's advertising was simple and direct, leaving the reader with the distinct impression of a 'no nonsense' company whose products spoke for themselves. However, in complete opposition to this general observation, the advertisement (6) which appeared on the cover of *Flight* in December 1968 is worthy of special mention. Not only was it almost heralding the final days of the company, but it is thought to be the last time an impressionist illustration was featured on the cover of this long-standing publication! The informed viewer may be able to track down component assemblies associated with the following thirty-seven Handley Page types:

Clive	HP 6	Hare	Manx
Gugnunc	HP 7	Harrow	Marathon
Halifax	HP 21	Hastings	O/400
Halton	HP 43	Hendon	O/700
Hamlet	HP 47	Heracles	Sapphire-Hastings
Hampden	HP 51	Herald	V/1500
Hampstead	HP 115	Hermes IV	Victor
Handcross	HPR 2	Heyford	W8
Hanley	Hyderabad	Hinaidi	
Hannibal	Jetstream		

1

HERMES — for the Empire air routes

Fastest British Airliner
High-altitude Operation
Top Speed of 357 m.p.h.
3,500-mile Range
Payload of 7½ tons
Capacity up to 63 Seats

HANDLEY PAGE

HANDLEY PAGE LIMITED, LONDON, ENGLAND

2

BRITAIN HAS WORLD'S FIRST OPERATIONAL CRESCENT BOMBER

Four-jet H P 80 Flies
Fastest Farthest and Highest

HANDLEY PAGE   LONDON · RADLETT · READING

3

BEST WISHES TO THE CREW OF THE R.N.Z.A.F. HASTINGS AND THEIR FELLOW COMPETITORS IN THE ENGLAND NEW ZEALAND AIR RACE FROM

HANDLEY PAGE

RADLETT   LONDON   READING

4

FASTEST · FARTHEST · HIGHEST

V *for* **VICTOR**

The rapid output of crescent-winged Victors, Britain's newest bombers, for the Royal Air Force has followed from the use of advanced structural and production techniques.

HANDLEY PAGE   RADLETT · LONDON · READING

We've flown together now for fifty years

Handley Page joined the Royal Air Force at the start — and its progenitors before that. Handley Page has been on active service ever since with a steady stream of famous aircraft... from the world's first successful heavy bombers, the big H.P. 0/400s and V/1500s of 1914/18... to the Hampdens and Halifaxes that gave Britain more than forty per cent of its offensive air power in the last war... and on to the massive Victor V-bombers of today.

Handley Page has a double reason for celebration — the RAF's half-century of splendid achievement and its own fifty years of unbroken service with the RAF.

5

FLIGHT-DECK DISPLAYS

FLIGHT International
incorporating AEROPLANE

All the best for 1969 from all the best of Handley Page

Aviation pioneer for 60 years

HANDLEY PAGE LTD., ST. ALBANS, HERTS, ENGLAND.

6

1   *Flight*, 18 June 1948.
2   *Flight*, 9 January 1953.
3   *The Aeroplane*, 9 October 1953.
4   *The Aeroplane*, 12 October 1956.
5   *Flight*, 28 March 1968.
6   *Flight*, 26 December 1968.

HAWKER AIRCRAFT LIMITED

Although several schemes and projects were considered and in some cases tendered, Hawker never produced a multi-engined aircraft that entered service. What the company did do, however, was to produce an almost unbroken succession of single-engined machines, invariably fighters, that served the RAF and countless foreign air forces for forty years. The Hawker name then carried on for a further seventeen years until 1977, when Hawker Siddeley Aviation Limited was merged into the newly formed British Aerospace plc. Hawker's best known post-war products were undoubtedly the Sea Fury, Sea Hawk and the Hunter, but its range of research prototypes, such as the P1040, P1052, P1072 and P1081, were also familiar to knowledgeable Farnborough air show crowds in the late 1940s and early 1950s. The Harrier, it should be added here, was later more associated with Hawker Siddeley, despite its design originating with Sir Sydney Camm's team as the Hawker P1127.

As with Gloster, Fairey and Blackburn, Hawker's appeal to the public relied upon forceful images with, where appropriate, the eye-catching inclusion of a naval vessel. It is interesting today to note the friendly support being given by hill tribesmen to the Iraqi Air Force Furies flying reassuringly low overhead!

Sea Fury

HAWKER AIRCRAFT

1

Hawker Fury
(Bristol Centaurus Engine)

HAWKER AIRCRAFT
BRANCH OF HAWKER SIDDELEY
AIRCRAFT COMPANY LIMITED

2

1   *Flight*, 30 January 1947.
2   *Flight*, 19 June 1947.

3

4

5

3   *The Aeroplane,* 16 June 1952.
4   *Flight,* 9 January 1953.
5   *Flight,* 13 September 1957.

MILES AIRCRAFT LIMITED

Although having produced entirely worthy post-war designs such as the Aerovan and Gemini, shown tastefully advertised here, the company found itself facing serious problems in the austere light aircraft market and was forced into liquidation within two years of the war's end. However, the Ministry of Supply, aware of the tempting production order for the firm's more ambitious Marathon feeder-liner for use both within and outside the United Kingdom, was anxious to keep the Miles organisation intact. Accordingly, Handley Page (Reading) Limited was formed to take over the aircraft assets and thus honour the contract.

After very surprisingly being contracted to design and build a supersonic research aircraft, the Miles M.52, only to have it cancelled in January 1946, Miles' presence on the post-war scene was, unfortunately, very short lived.

1   *Flight,* c.1946.
2   *Flight,* c.1947.
3   *The Aeroplane,*
         13 June 1947.

SAFETY . . . THE MILES MARATHON . . . FIRST BRITISH AEROPLANE DESIGNED TO MEET THE SAFETY REQUIREMENTS OF THE PROVISIONAL INTERNATIONAL CIVIL AVIATION ORGANISATION

1

MILES AEROVAN . . . The "one-tonner" of the air. Maximum range 800 miles. Cruising speed 112 m.p.h. Freight capacity 530 cu. ft. In operation as freighter, 9-seater passenger plane, livestock transport. Also available as caravan, flying showroom, workshop, ambulance, etc.

2

MILES GEMINI . . . the safest light aircraft in the world. Maximum speed 150 m.p.h. . . . range 820 miles . . . stalling speed 35 m.p.h. . . . take-off run 150 yards. Unexcelled single engine characteristics.

MILES AIRCRAFT LIMITED READING ENGLAND

3

PERCIVAL AIRCRAFT LIMITED, HUNTING PERCIVAL AIRCRAFT LIMITED

Percival's 1946 advertisement announcing the arrival of the Merganser may as well have announced its imminent departure. Only one prototype was built and the aircraft failed to win any orders in the small airliner/freight carrier field. More success was had by the Prince-President-Pembroke series of medium transports, and by the Prentice, Provost and Jet Provost trainers for the RAF.

In April 1954, the company changed its name to Hunting Percival Aircraft Limited and later, in 1957, to Hunting Aircraft Limited, thus finally losing sight of what had long been a family name hallmark within British aviation.

Although Percival's immediate post-war advertising appears rather drab and uninspiring, later samples showing Hunting Percival at work are certainly vibrant and suggest a more invigorated company.

1   *The Aeroplane*, 10 May 1946.
2   *The Aeroplane*, 14 May 1948.
3   *Flight*, 30 August 1957.
4   *Flight*, 29 August 1958.
5   *The Aeroplane*, 31 August 1958.
6   Source uncertain, *c*.1980.

4

5

6

PILATUS BRITTEN-NORMAN

Britten-Norman is one of the few firms that have managed to escape being drawn into the amalgamated mass of companies that now constitute BAe Systems. Located on the Isle of Wight, it follows other pioneering organisations such as Samuel J. Wight and Saunders-Roe in upholding British aviation skills. It was John Britten and Desmond Norman who, in the early 1960s, identifying the need for simple robust utility aircraft, produced first the Islander and subsequently (in 1970) the Tri-islander, largely in competition with the Short Skyvan.

The original company underwent several name changes in the 1970s, before emerging as Pilatus Britten-Norman and finally, in 1998, as Britten-Norman Limited yet again. Perhaps symptomatic of the new age is this 1995 example of photographic image advertising for the Defender, the military version of the Islander – undoubtedly forthright in its message, but more clinically observant rather than artistic in its appeal.

1

1   International Air Tattoo programme, 1995.

1   *The Aeroplane*, 25 January 1946.
2   *Aeronautics*, December 1946.

PORTSMOUTH AVIATION LIMITED

In 1943, the Portsmouth, Southsea and Isle of Wight Company changed its name to become the more manageable Portsmouth Aviation Limited. It then went on to repair and flight-test some 5,000 aircraft before the end of the war. Following this, the company undertook the design and prototype manufacture of the twin-engine, twin-boom Aerocar, but despite negotiations for production in India that appeared hopeful, this promising design failed to mature. Although no longer engaging in basic design projects, the company is still producing equipment for Britain's defence market.

The company's advertising in 1946 showed an advanced, attractive aeroplane which, like so many other contemporary designs, fell foul of very restrictive commercial pressures.

1   **2**

For complete flying training the

DESFORD

sets a new world standard in light aeroplanes

REID AND SIGRIST LIMITED

Fred Sigrist, co-founder of the company, was a hard-driving individual who, with T.O.M. Sopwith, had created H.G. Hawker Engineering Company Limited and, soon after, Hawker Aircraft Limited.

Reid and Sigrist Limited was formed in 1928 and continued until 1953, during which time two original trainer designs, the improbably named R.S.I. 'Snargasher' and the R.S.3 Desford, flew in prototype form only. The Desford, however, went on after modifications to provide useful service as a prone-pilot research aircraft.

Despite its promising claims in somewhat prosaic advertising, the company, better known for its aircraft instruments, never achieved front rank status as an airframe constructor.

SAUNDERS-ROE LIMITED

Saunders-Roe could rightly claim to have been a leading British aircraft manufacturer with many excellent innovative designs to its credit. In the post-war years however it followed several design paths that ultimately led to its demise. The first of these, the jet-propelled flying-boat fighter, resulted from what had seemed to be a most progressive wartime idea. The S.R.A/I was indeed later proven to be a high-performance machine, certainly when measured against contemporary waterborne aircraft standards, but the project fell by the wayside when shown to be outpaced by the new generation of land-based fighters.

The Princess flying-boat, in a class by itself for elegance, was thought to be a natural choice for BOAC's transatlantic routes. The airline, however, had other ideas and although manufacture commenced on three prototypes, only one took the skies before BOAC, in 1952, declared its interest at an end. Although consideration was given by the RAF for trooping duties and a suggestion that the aircraft be used as a flying test-bed for atomic reactors promised an extended flying life, practical work on this magnificent machine came to an end in 1954.

1   *The Aeroplane,* 10 May 1946.

1   *The Aeroplane,* 28 March 1946.
2   *Flight,* 12 June 1947.

The third line of development that ended in disappointment for Saunders-Roe was the rocket-powered fighter. The capture of German technical data at the end of the war had generated a high official regard for this type of high-rate climb interceptor. Therefore, in the early 1950s, with reliable British-designed rocket propulsion units now available, Saunders-Roe went ahead with what became the S.R.53. Highly successful flight-test work on this new concept led to a 'fully operational' development, the P.177, but as so often happened, what promised to be an advanced aeroplane well ahead of its time, with clear expectations of significant export sales, failed to materialise. The Ministry of Supply withdrew funding in 1958.

Despite all the commercial and political uncertainties, the company's advertising support was superb. If this alone could have sold the firm's products, there would indeed have been little to worry about. Saunders-Roe was a visionary company that was dealt a very unkind hand by fate, for if but one of its design concepts (including its involvement with the revolutionary hovercraft) had gone fully to plan, its future would have been very different. One aspect of change did, however, have a positive impact upon the company, for, having taken over Cierva to form the Saunders-Roe Helicopter Division at Eastleigh, the firm then developed and produced the Skeeter and other projects before the final takeover by Westland.

4   *The Aeroplane,* 14 May 1948.
5   *The Aeroplane,* 14 April 1950.
6   *The Aeroplane,* 23 April 1948.
7   *The Aeroplane,* 11 June 1948.
8   *The Aeroplane,* 7 September 1951.
9   *Flight,* 9 January 1953.
10 *The Aeroplane,* 14 September 1956.

4

5

6

7

8

"SKEETERS" for the Army . . .

designed and built by

SAUNDERS-ROE

The "SKEETER" Mk.6 has been chosen by the Army

for A.O.P. and light liaison duties

9

CONSTANT AIR PATROL

SAUNDERS ROE LTD

WORKS AT:— EAST COWES, ISLE OF WIGHT   EASTLEIGH, SOUTHAMPTON   BEAUMARIS, ANGLESEY

10

SCOTTISH AVIATION LIMITED

Although formed in the wartime years, it was the short take-off and landing capabilities of, firstly, the single-engined Pioneer, and then the Twin Pioneer, that brought the firm to wider notice after the war. Scottish Aviation subsequently expanded to acquire the design authority for several previously independent companies, including Phillips and Powis/Miles Aircraft and, via Beagle, Auster Limited and Taylorcraft Aeroplanes (England) Limited. In 1978, the company ceased to exist, having entered the one-way system called British Aerospace.

1 *Flight,* 10 September 1954.
2 *The Aeroplane,* 10 May 1957.

SHORT BROTHERS LIMITED/ SHORT BROS & HARLAND LIMITED

Shorts, who effectively started the British aircraft manufacturing industry, is, remarkably, still a well-respected name within the aviation world. Although the concept of very large flying-boats was soon shown to be flawed in the early 1950s, civil variants of the wartime Sunderland, such as Hythe, Seaford, Sandringham and Solent, along with the twin-engined Sealand, proved successful until the end of the decade. The Shetland advertised here and produced in collaboration with Saunders-Roe prototype form for military and civil use had a wingspan of 150ft – edging toward that of the Saunders-Roe Princess' span of 209ft!

Short Bros & Harland Limited formed in 1947 and, now entirely based in Belfast, also undertook work on a miscellany of types that ranged from the tailless Sherpa aerodynamic research vehicle and the S.B.5 used for assessing low-speed handling with excessive wing sweep-angles, to the Sperrin with its four engines unusually mounted in vertical pairs, the Seamew anti-submarine aircraft, the S.C.I Short Vertical Take-Off machine and the Belfast, Skyvan and SD330/360 range of heavy and light transports.

1 *Flight,* 20 September 1945.
2 *The Aeroplane,* 18 January 1946.

3   *Flight,* 24 January 1946.
4   *The Aeroplane,* 10 May 1946.
5   *The Aeroplane,* 23 November 1951.

The *Short* SC.1 goes forward

The recent dramatically successful demonstrations on seven successive days at Farnborough by the Short SC.1 proved conclusively to the world that Shorts have achieved a major break-through in aeronautical progress. With smooth and effortless transition from jet-borne hovering to wing-borne flight and vice versa now a routine operation, the way to pure jet VTOL military and civil aircraft of the future can be clearly seen.

Developed by Shorts under a Ministry of Aviation research contract, the SC.1 has four Rolls-Royce RB.108 jet engines mounted vertically for lift, with a fifth at the tail for propulsion. A Short-designed auto-stabiliser system gives automatically controlled stability during hovering and transition. No other aircraft achieves VTOL in this way. No other aircraft has brought high performance VTOL to the stage of immediate application to aviation's everyday needs. And no other team has developed so much of the practical equipment which will be needed in the VTOL aircraft of tomorrow.

AT **Shorts** IDEAS TAKE SHAPE **on time**

SHORT BROTHERS & HARLAND LIMITED
Queens Island   Belfast   Northern Ireland
The first manufacturers of aircraft in the world

6

There's a worldwide need for an all-purpose, robust, light freighter with good short field performance and the ability to carry a wide range of 2-ton loads.
So Shorts built the Skyvan with nearly twice the capacity of any comparable aeroplane.

SHORT BROTHERS & HARLAND LTD.
LONDON AND BELFAST

7

THE LONG AND
THE SHORT OF IT

Two distinguished newcomers to the air transport scene.
The giant **Belfast** — first strategic freighter for R.A.F. Transport Command.
The Versatile **Turbo-Skyvan** — robust, light freighter with outstanding short-field performance.

SHORT BROTHERS & HARLAND LTD.
LONDON AND BELFAST

8

6   *Aeronautics*, February 1961.
7   Source uncertain, *c.*1965.
8   Source uncertain, *c.*1968.
9   *Flight International*, 16 April 1977.

How to keep your passengers in the style and luxury they're accustomed to.
And do it economically.

Airline passengers enjoy luxury these days.

Flying between big cities in the new generation jet liners they have become accustomed to that spacious wide-bodied environment, with all the comforts of home – plus a pretty stewardess to serve the drinks

It's the sort of treatment that makes them downright discontented when they leave the big jets and step into the mundane world of normal commuter flying – narrow aisles, tight packed seating, no headroom, no galley – and no stewardess.

However better times are on the way for them. Shorts SD3-30's are now in service or are entering service with the world's leading Commuter Airlines

This unique wide-bodied 30-seat commuter has been designed to accommodate your passengers in the style they've grown accustomed to. Luxury seating, wide aisle, walk-about headroom, washroom facilities, panoramic windows, overhead lockers, a galley – and provision for a stewardess! Just some of the features that combine with low initial and low operating costs to make this super quiet airliner the commuter you and your passengers have been waiting for.

Standardise on SD3-30 – and your passengers will label you as their Airline who cares about them.

DLT.
LUFTVERKEHRSGESELLSCHAFT
of Frankfurt, Germany.

SHORTS Aircraft and Missiles

SD3-30

LIAISON OFFICES

USA MAIN OFFICE
(East Coast)
Shorts Aircraft
Logan International Airport
Boston, Mass 02128
Tel: (617) 569 6110
Telex: 710 329 0325

USA REGIONAL OFFICE
110 Newport Drive
Suite 200 Newport Beach
California 92660
Tel: (714) 644 8975
Telex: 230 678 360

AUSTRALIA
(Region Office)
Shorts Airservices Pty Ltd
Challenger House
15/17 Young Street
Sydney 2000, NSW Australia
Tel: Sydney 27-3275 Cable: Airshort

Airport Road, Belfast, Northern Ireland
Tel: 0232 58444   Telex: 74688

9

VICKERS-ARMSTRONG LIMITED

Vickers–Armstrong's contribution to Britain's post-war aviation industry was immense. Although the single-seat fighters from Spitfire to Swift and Scimitar were considered to be Supermarine designs, the company was now officially regarded as Vickers–Armstrong (Aircraft) Limited – Supermarine Works!

Vickers–Armstrong Limited, Aircraft Section, based at Weybridge, was far more concerned with bomber and transport projects. The Viking airliner, clearly a descendant of the Wellington and Warwick aircraft, proved a useful post-war stop-gap for domestic passenger services before the arrival of the turboprop Viscount in 1954. The Valiant, the first British 'V' bomber to enter service, also later equipped the RAF's first dedicated air tanker squadron (No.214) before major structural problems caused the type to be withdrawn in January 1965. Although the Vanguard and V.C.10 were not produced in large numbers, both types performed well in airline use, with the V.C.10 going on to perform transport and tanking duties with the RAF.

In 1960, Vickers joined English Electric, Bristol and Hunting Aircraft in forming the British Aircraft Corporation, whereupon the company's expertise, led by Sir George Edwards, played a vital part in the BAC 1-11, T.S.R.2 and Concorde projects. Vicker's post-war advertising, judged by this selection of samples, certainly 'held its own' when compared to that of other major companies, but might be regarded as 'workman-like' rather than artistically inspired.

1 *Aircraft of the Fighting Powers* vol. VI (1945).
2 Submarine brochure, *c.*1946.
3 *The Aeroplane*, 21 October 1955.
4 RAF Flying Review, *c.*1956.
5 RAF Tangmere 'At home' souvenir book, 19 September 1959.

WESTLAND AIRCRAFT LIMITED

Though now a subsidiary of the Italian Finmeccanica group and teamed with Agusta, Westland, at the time of writing, remains one of only two British aircraft manufacturing companies (Shorts being the other) to have retained its basic identity from the First World War. The Wyvern naval torpedo-carrying aircraft made tortuous progress in becoming the company's only post-war, fixed-wing venture, eighty-seven eventually emerging as the S.MK4 production variant. However, when the company's long tradition of conventional machines came to an end, a new era began with the firm's entry into the rotary-wing field. This first took the form of a licence being granted by the American United Aircraft Corporation for the assembly of Sikorsky S-51 helicopters powered by a British Alvis Leonides engine. From this beginning, in 1947, the company has gone from strength to strength, with many successful designs, civil and military, to its credit. It is not within the scope of this book to expand upon the growth of the company, but the separate formation in 1967 of Normalair-Garrett Limited, and its advertising to exploit environmental control equipment, is worthy of individual recognition (in the Equipment Providers section).

Westland's transition from fixed- to rotary-wing aircraft manufacturer was certainly captured in its advertising, space permitting but a few samples to be shown here.

1 *Aircraft of the Fighting Powers* vol. VI (1945).
2 *Flight*, 22 June 1951.
3 *Flight*, 19 June 1953.
4 *The Aeroplane*, 3 September 1956.

1

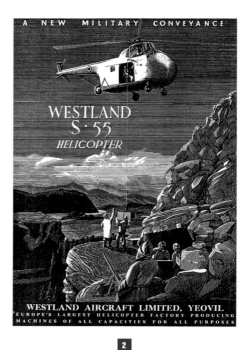

2

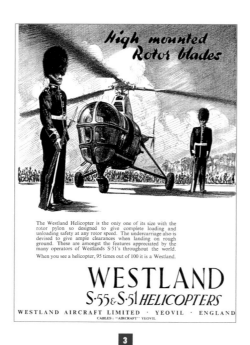

3

4

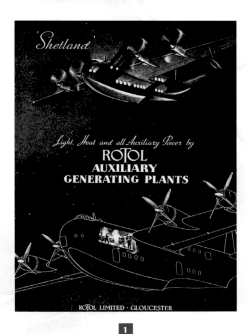

THE ENGINE MAKERS

Although the makers of famous aeroplanes can usually be instantly recalled, the names of the engine manufacturers sometimes require a little additional memory searching. This selection of advertisements is therefore aimed at bringing again to mind the great British aero-engine firms of the post-war period.

Armstrong Siddeley's Python gas turbine, fitted with Rotol propellers, appeared to be the chosen powerplant for whatever large post-war project was being considered, but it was only ever fitted to the Wyvern naval strike fighter. Nonetheless, the ambitious advertising was certainly impressive!

Alvis was second to none in promoting its famed Leonides radial piston engine for both fixed and rotary-winged machines, frequently employing the much sought after artist Frank Wootton to great effect.

Napier, de Havilland Engines, Bristol, Metropolitan-Vickers and Blackburn were all well known and respected companies before the squeeze of rationalization took hold. All have now passed into history, leaving only Rolls-Royce to carry Britain's traditional aero-engine skills forward. The company's advertising style has always been dignified but, as with that of most firms, it has now become more confined to a website rather than the popular aviation press.

1   *Flight*, 17 May 1945.
2   *The Aeroplane*, 9 November 1945.
3   *The Aeroplane*, 4 January 1945.
4   *The Aeroplane*, 31 January 1947.

5

6

7

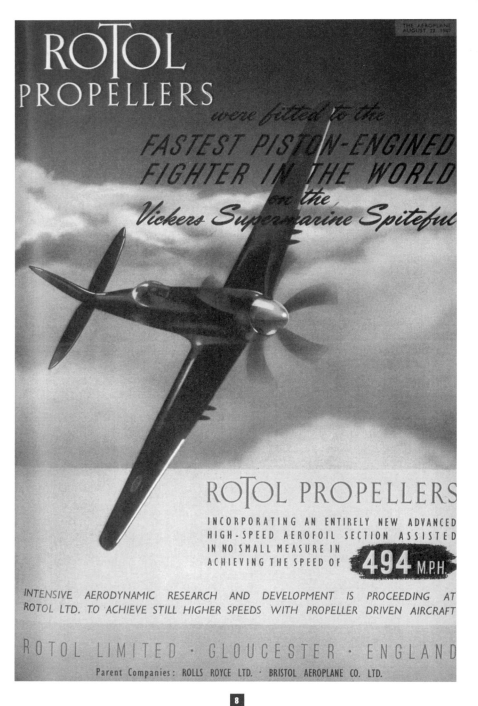

8

5   *Flight*, 29 May 1947.
6   *Flight*, 5 June 1947.
7   *Flight*, 26 June 1947.
8   *The Aeroplane*, 22 August 1947.

9

10

12

11

9 *Flight*, 2 September 1948.
10 *The Aeroplane*, 4 September 1953.
11 *The Aeroplane*, 22 January 1954.
12 *The Aeroplane*, 14 September 1956.

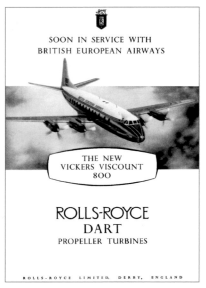

SOON IN SERVICE WITH
BRITISH EUROPEAN AIRWAYS

THE NEW
VICKERS VISCOUNT
800

ROLLS-ROYCE
DART
PROPELLER TURBINES

ROLLS-ROYCE LIMITED, DERBY, ENGLAND

13

In Service with the Royal Navy

The Alvis Leonides Major has been
chosen to power the Westland
Whirlwind helicopters now being
delivered to the Royal Navy.

ALVIS LEONIDES Aero Engines

ALVIS LIMITED · COVENTRY · ENGLAND

14

ROLLS-ROYCE
AVON TURBO JETS
power the
ENGLISH ELECTRIC P.I.Bs
FOR THE ROYAL AIR FORCE

~CROSS~

15

Some famous King's Cup winners who enjoyed the full-throttle reliability of their Gipsies.

1928 GIPSY MOTH	WALLY HOPE
1932 FOX MOTH	WALLY HOPE
1933 LEOPARD MOTH	de H
1935 FALCON SIX	TOMMY ROSE
1936 VEGA GULL	CHARLES E. GARDNER
1937 MEW GULL	CHARLES E. GARDNER
1938 MEW GULL	ALEX HENSHAW
1949 GEMINI	NAT SOMERS
1950 HAWK TRAINER	EDDIE DAY
1953 CHIPMUNK	PAT FILLINGHAM
1955 MEW GULL	PETER CLIFFORD
1956 AUSTER ALPHA	JIMMY DENYER

THE DE HAVILLAND ENGINE COMPANY LIMITED

LEAVESDEN, HERTFORDSHIRE

16

17

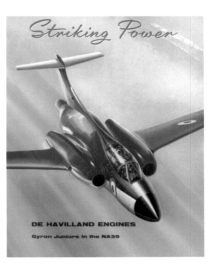

18

19

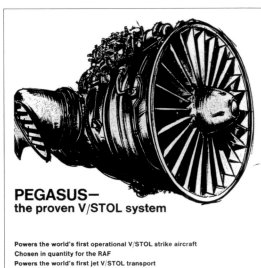

20

13 *The Aeroplane*, 18 January 1957.

14 *Flight*, 6 September 1957.

15 *Flight*, 6 September 1957.

16 *Flight*, 4 July 1958.

17 *The Aeroplane*, 20 August 1958.

18 *The Aeroplane*, 28 November 1958.

19 Source uncertain, *c.*1958.

20 *RAFA magazine*, 18 June 1966.

THE FUEL AND OIL COMPANIES

Esso, Shell and Castrol have largely dominated the supply of fuel and lubricants for aircraft since well before the Second World War. This interesting group of illustrations reveals again the pre-eminence of Frank Wootton in portraying what might be thought of as 'everyday products' in a dynamic framework. The naval environment, i.e. the aircraft carrier, and a night-time setting are just two artistic ingredients which, enhanced by Wootton's genius, are still guaranteed to capture the imagination!

1

2

3

4

1 *The Aeroplane*, 23 June 1950.
2 *The Aeroplane*, 21 December 1951.
3 Source uncertain, *c.*1954.
4 Source uncertain, *c.*1957.
5 International Air Tattoo programme, 1995.
6 International Air Tattoo programme, 1995.

5

6

1

2

THE PAINT AND FINISH SUPPLIERS

Though it may seem logical to include the 'paint and finish' suppliers in the Equipment and Providers section, the special nature of their products deserves separate recognition. Both Cellon and Titanine ensured that the artistic support was colourful, evocative and fully in keeping with the advanced aviation projects of the immediate post-war period.

1   *Aircraft of the Fighting Powers* vol. VI (1945).
2   *The Aeroplane,* 9 November 1945.

T.T. SIX Satin Finish scheme has been world-renowned since the earliest days of flying, for protecting and beautifying Club and private owner-type aircraft.

TITANINE

TITANINE LTD., COLINDALE, LONDON, N.W.9   Tel.: COLindale 8123 (6 lines)

WHEREVER SURFACES REQUIRE PROTECTION 'CELLON' CAN PROVIDE THE FINIS

CELLON PROTECTIVE FINISHES
for Air, Sea & Land Transport

3   *The Aeroplane, c.*1946.
4   *The Aeroplane, c.* March 1947.
5   *The Aeroplane,* 4 July 1947.

CELLON
AIRCRAFT FINISHES

6

T. T. NINE—The new featherweight finish for beautifying and protecting all surfaces of metal aircraft—Total deposited weight less than one ounce per square yard.

TITANINE

7

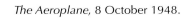

The de Havilland Venom is Finished with—
TITANINE
Materials

TITANINE LIMITED · COLINDALE · LONDON · N.W.9   Telephone: COLindale 8/33 (4 lines)
Associated Companies: Titanine Inc., U.S.A.; N.Y. Titanine, Holland; Vernici, Titanine, Italy.

8

6   *The Aeroplane*, 8 October 1948.
7   *The Aeroplane*, 7 December 1948.
8   *The Aeroplane*, 30 June 1950.

THE GENERAL EQUIPMENT PROVIDERS

The large number of airframe and engine manufacturers already referred to is only exceeded by the wide range of specialist system, component and service suppliers. Varied they certainly were, with heavy duty forging factories running alongside cotton bag makers, but all proving necessary in the supply of a finished aeroplane. To identify all the contributing companies would be well beyond the scope of this section which aims, no doubt with only limited success, to give a typical cross-section of those most influentially involved. Advertising styles clearly extended from the dramatic to the prosaic, but whatever a company's speciality, a talented artist was usually striving behind the scenes to create a unique and personal impression of the product. Discussions with contemporary ex-employees often raised the question: 'Do you remember the Desoutter managing director adverts?' The answer is 'Yes', and they are recalled here with amusement, and some affection! Also included is an advert from Tinkertex which, though understandably acceptable to an earlier generation, would not, in all probability, pass today's sexist standards! (Shame!).

The manufacturing companies, both big and small, which formed the British aviation industry constitute a very long list indeed. It is hoped that their vital contributions have been fairly represented here.

1   *Aircraft of the Fighting Powers* vol. VI (1945).
2   *Flight*, 28 February 1946.
3   *The Aeroplane*, 1 March 1946.
4   *Aircraft of the Fighting Powers* vol. VII (1946).

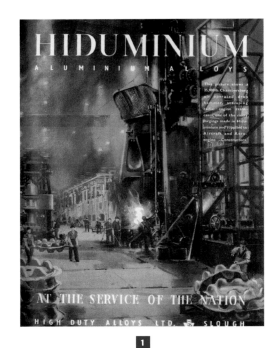

1

2

3

4

5

REFUELLING IN FLIGHT...

6

7

8

9

5 *Flight*, 9 January 1947.
6 *Flight*, 20 March 1947.
7 *Flight*, 27 March 1947.
8 *Flight*, 15 May 1947.
9 *The Aeroplane*, 1 August 1947.

10

11

12

13

10   *The Aeroplane,* 16 April 1948.
11   *The Aeroplane,* 23 April 1948.
12   *The Aeroplane,* 14 May 1948.
13   *The Aeroplane,* 25 June 1948.

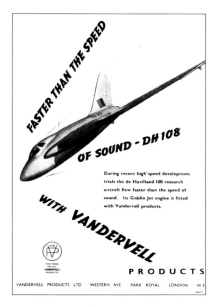

One of the de Havilland Doves owned by the Anglo-Iranian Oil Company and operated by Airwork Ltd., in flight over the refineries at Abadan

14 *The Aeroplane*, 8 October 1948.
15 *The Aeroplane*, 26 November 1948.
16 *The Aeroplane*, 17 December 1948.
17 Source uncertain, *c*.1949.

18

19

20

21

22

18   Source uncertain, *c.*1949.
19   *The Aeroplane*, 9 June 1950.
20   *The Aeroplane*, 20 June 1950.
21   *Flight*, 9 January 1953.
22   *Flight*, 17 July 1953.

23

24

25

26

27

23   Source uncertain, *c.*1953.
24   *The Aeroplane*, 4 September 1953.
25   *The Aeroplane*, 10 September 1954.
26   *The Aeroplane*, 31 August 1956.
27   *The Aeroplane*, 14 September 1956.

Before building Concorde they came to us for guidance

25 years' experience on powered flying controls with
25 million unit flying hours on civil and military aircraft.

DOWTY
Dowty Group, Cheltenham, England

28

POWER FLYING CONTROLS

by

Hobson

selected for the Gloster Javelin

Many of Britain's leading aircraft designers are now specifying Hobson Power Flying Controls for operation of the primary control surfaces, including "All-Flying" or "Slab" tailplanes. The duplicated hydraulically operated single screw jack unit, as illustrated, is typical of Hobson units fitted to the Gloster Javelin.

H. M. HOBSON LTD · FORDHOUSES · WOLVERHAMPTON

29

breaking new barriers
with
**DOWTY
EQUIPMENT**

The Bristol T188 includes a Dowty fuel control system, undercarriages, flying controls and high temperature hydraulics.

DOWTY GROUP LIMITED · CHELTENHAM · ENGLAND

30

28   *Flight,* 13 April 1971.
29   *Flight,* 14 February 1958.
30   *Flight,* 3 May 1962.

31 International Air Tattoo programme, 1995.

32 International Air Tattoo programme, 1995.

33 International Air Tattoo programme, 1995.

34 Cobham website, 2007.

THE AIRLINES

British South American Airways, British Overseas Airways Corporation and British European Airways represented the main British flag-carriers in the immediate post-war airline market.

Perhaps mindful of its Imperial Airways heritage and, of course, well aware that (unlike the manufacturing companies) it needed to attract a large volume of customers, BOAC lost little time in setting the pace with advertisements having a wide public appeal. Although the years just after the war remained bleak for most of Britain's population, the airlines' colourful campaigns proved seductive indeed to both travellers and non-travellers alike.

1 BOAC poster, 1946.
2 BSAA poster, *c.*1947.

3   BOAC poster, *c.*1948.
4   BOAC poster, *c.*1949.

5   BOAC poster, 1950.
6   BOAC poster, 1953.

7

8

7　*The Aeroplane,* 31 August 1956.
8　Farnborough '64 publication.

THE AIR SHOWS

In bringing this book to a close, it is perhaps appropriate to include just a sample of the 'glamour ads' that have, over the years, announced the airshow spectaculars – many of which rely on vintage or restored examples of aircraft already well recalled within these pages!

Best remembered with nostalgic affection are the air displays which have formed part of every post-war SBAC Farnborough exhibition. When these first commenced in 1948, the demonstration of so many new prototypes – British prototypes – undoubtedly provided a show guaranteed to empty the marquee housing a range of specialist equipment on stands that were distinctly 'low-key'. Today, however, the flying demonstrations are generally of a 'corporate', more straightforward nature, complementing what has now become an immensely impressive international technological showcase. But whilst the nature of flying at Farnborough may have changed, the excellent air shows promoted by the Flying Legends at Duxford, the Shuttleworth Collection at Old Warden, the Royal International Air Tattoo at Fairford and the Royal Air force Association at Jersey and elsewhere, to name but a few, are invariably well organised events that provide an annual wealth of nostalgic and modern day aerial entertainment. Long may they continue!

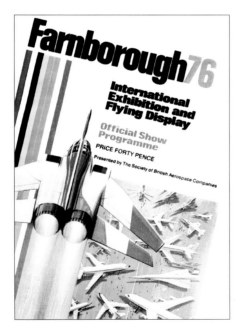

9   SBAC Display programme, 1950.
10 Farnborough programme, 1961.
11 Farnborough programme, 1976.
12 Farnborough programme, 1988.

INDEX TO PRINCIPAL AIRCRAFT CONSTRUCTORS AND ENGINE MAKER ADVERTISEMENTS